Nurturing
Informed Thinking

Nurturing
Informed Thinking

Reading, Talking, and Writing
Across Content-Area Sources

SUNDAY CUMMINS

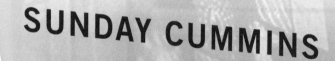

HEINEMANN
Portsmouth, NH

Heinemann
361 Hanover Street
Portsmouth, NH 03801–3912
www.heinemann.com

Offices and agents throughout the world

The author and publisher wish to thank those who have generously given permission to reprint borrowed material:

Figure 1.1a–b: Cover and excerpt from *Trapped! A Whale's Rescue* by Robert Burleigh, illustrations by Wendell Minor. Text copyright © 2015 by Robert Burleigh. Illustrations copyright © 2015 by Wendell Minor. Published by Charlesbridge Publishing Inc. Reprinted by permission of the Publisher. *(continued on page viii)*

Cataloging-in-Publication Data is on file at the Library of Congress.

ISBN: 978-0-325-09283-6

Acquisitions Editor: Tobey Antao
Production Editor: Sean Moreau
Cover and Interior Designs: Suzanne Heiser
Typesetter: Shawn Girsberger
Manufacturing: Steve Bernier

Printed in the United States of America on acid-free paper

22 21 20 19 18 VP 1 2 3 4 5

CONTENTS

4

Supporting: *Instructional* Moves That Help Students 80

5

Releasing Responsibility: Student-Led Research with Inquiry Charts and Other Scaffolds 113

CREDITS FOR *NURTURING INFORMED THINKING* (continued from page iv)

COVER

Earbuds: © Getty Images, Banar Fil Ardhi / EyeEm

Bookshelf: © Getty Images, clu

Infographic: © Getty Images, Aunt Spray

Web: © Getty Images, Tetra Images

Videos: © Getty Images, Vertigo 3D / Daniel Melekhin

Camper: © Getty Images, Christopher Murray / EyeEm

Newspapers: © Shutterstock, ernstc

Lusitania: © Shutterstock, Everett Historical.

TEXT

Page 2: Excerpt from *The College, Career, and Civic Life (C3) Framework for Social Studies State Standards: Guidance for Enhancing the Rigor of K–12 Civics, Economics, Geography, and History.* Published in 2013 by the National Council for Social Studies, Silver Spring, MD.

Figure 1.2: Excerpt from "Daring Rescue of Whale off Farallones / Humpback Nuzzled Her Saviors in Thanks after They Untangled Her from Crab Lines, Diver Says" by Peter Fimrite from *SFGate*, December 14, 2005. Published 2005 by SFGate.

Figure 2.1: NGSS Lead States. 2013. *Next Generation Science Standards: For States, By State*s. Washington, DC: The National Academies Press.

Page 18: Excerpt from *Reflections: Ancient Civilizations* by Harcourt School Publishers. Copyright © 2007 by Harcourt School Publishers. Published by Harcourt School Publishers.

Page 18: "8 Reasons It Wasn't Easy Being Spartan" by Evan Andrews from History.com, March 5, 2013. Published 2013 by A&E Networks LLC.

Figure 2.2: Excerpt from *My Brother Martin: A Sister Remembers Growing Up with Rev. Dr. Martin Luther King Jr.* by Christine King Farris. Copyright © 2003 by Christine King Farris. Published by Simon & Schuster Books for Young Readers.

Figure 2.4: Excerpt from *Delivering Justice: W.W. Law and the Fight for Civil Rights* by Jim Haskins. Copyright © 2005 by Jim Haskins. Published by Candlewick Press.

Figure 2.5: Excerpt from: Wonderopolis® article: *Can You Ride a Sound Wave?* (http://wonderopolis .org/wonder/can-you-ride-a-sound-wave). Wonderopolis is created by the National Center for Families Learning (NCFL).

Figure 3.1: Excerpt from "A strategy for previewing textbooks: Teaching readers to become THIEVES" by Suzanne Liff Manz from *The Reading Teacher,* Vol. 55, No. 5, February 2002. Published by Wiley on behalf of the International Literacy Association.

Figure 3.4: Excerpt from *Algonquins: Native Americans* by Sarah Tieck. Published 2014 by Big Buddy Books. Reprinted by permission of Abdo Publishing.

Figure 3.6: "Cracking down on the illegal ivory market is key to saving elephants" by Daniel Stiles, *The Guardian,* adapted by Newsela staff, https://newsela.com/read/save-elephants-plan/id/24303, November 29, 2016 was adapted from "Why it makes sense to burn ivory stockpiles" by Andrew Halliday and Paula Kahumbu from theguardian.com, April 23, 2016. Reprinted by permission of Newsela and Guardian News & Media Limited.

Figure 3.7: Adapted from "Saving Africa's Elephants," map by Jim McMahon. Published in *Scholastic News,* January 17, 2017. Copyright © 2017 by Scholastic Inc. Reprinted by permission.

Figure 3.9a–b: Adapted from "Another Earth" by Tricia Culligan. Published in *Scholastic News*, October 14, 2016. Copyright © 2016 by Scholastic Inc. Reprinted by permission.

Figure 3.10: "Proxima B Habitability" infographic courtesy of NASA's Goddard Flight Center/Mary Pat Hrybyk-Keith.

Figure 3.13a: Excerpt from *Simple Machines: Wheels, Levers, and Pulleys* by David Adler. Copyright © 2014 by David Adler. Published by Holiday House.

Figure 3.13b: Excerpt from *Machines Make It Move* by Stephen M. Tomecek. Copyright © 2002 National Geographic Society. Published by National Geographic Society.

Figure 3.14a: Excerpt from *Weather and Climate* by Rebecca L. Johnson. Copyright © 2002 by National Geographic Society. Published by National Geographic Society.

Figure 3.14b: Excerpt from: Wonderopolis® article: *Where Is Tornado Alley?* (http://wonderopolis .org/wonder/where-is-tornado-alley). Wonderopolis is created by the National Center for Families Learning (NCFL).

Figure 3.17: Excerpt from *Medieval Lives: Knight* by Moira Butterfield. Published 2009 by Franklin Watts Ltd.

Figure 3.18: Excerpt from *Le Morte D'Arthur: King Arthur and the Knights of the Round Table.* Copyright © 2015 Canterbury Classics. Published by Canterbury Classics.

Figure 3.21: Excerpt from *Seymour Simon's Extreme Oceans* by Seymour Simon. Copyright © 2013 by Seymour Simon. Published by Chronicle Books.

Figure 3.22: Excerpt from "The Storm: A First-Hand Account of Katrina" by Shilo Groover from *ByGeorge! GW's Faculty, Staff and Community Newspaper,* October 19, 2005. Published 2005 by George Washington University.

Figure 3.26a–b: Excerpt from: Wonderopolis® article: *How Can You Get a Bird's Eye View?* (http://wonderopolis.org/wonder/how-can-you-get-a-birds-eye-view). Wonderopolis is created by the National Center for Families Learning (NCFL).

Figure 3.27a–b: Adapted from "Drone Control." Published in *Scholastic News,* December 1, 2015. Copyright © 2015 by Scholastic Inc. Reprinted by permission.

Figure 5.11: Yahoo! search engine results for "grand canyon + weathering" obtained from https://search.yahoo.com.

Acknowledgments

I am immensely grateful to the many thought partners who helped me develop the ideas in this book.

When I first started thinking about this book, I had a lot of questions. I realized I needed to learn more before I could begin to write. I asked a principal at a local school if she knew a teacher who would work with me. She introduced me to Nicole Ballew. Nicole and her students welcomed me into their classroom, embraced my ideas, and turned them into rich learning opportunities. Soon we were all hooked on learning by reading, talking, and writing across sources. While I traveled to consult in other schools, Nicole continued this work, texting me enthusiastically along the way. We spent many Friday afternoons pouring over students' responses, asking questions about how to strengthen our practice, searching for sources, and planning new lessons. Thanks to Nicole, a kindred spirit in the classroom, ideas for this book began to evolve.

As I began to share what we were learning with others, several colleagues stepped forward and offered to help—Shannon, Micheline, Kelli, Meghan, Caleb, Kris, Martha, Karen, Chris, Anders, Emily, and Tara. We conferred in person, by phone, and by Skype; they tried out lessons and then sent me feedback with lots of photos of student work, anchor charts, and other instructional artifacts they'd created. Over time, thanks to these amazing educators, the ideas for this book began to take root, and I realized I was ready to write.

There is one more thought partner I'd like to acknowledge—Tobey Antao, my editor at Heinemann. I first spoke with Tobey early in this journey—the spring of 2015. The more I talked with Tobey, the more I realized I needed to get back into a classroom and try out some ideas. When I shared this, she agreed. At that moment, I honestly thought I had lost the opportunity to propose a book to Heinemann. Then Tobey surprised me by asking if we could schedule a call for the next fall. By the time she called me the following October, I had started working with Nicole. Every month Tobey checked in to see how things were going, and the next spring we created a book proposal. When the proposal was accepted, Tobey scheduled a slew of due dates to keep me on track, read drafts of chapters, and provided feedback that made my writing stronger. I am forever grateful to Tobey for her commitment to making this book happen.

Finally, while they are not colleagues in the field, I also want to share my gratitude to "Team Cummins." Stephen, my husband and soulmate, always believes I will figure out what to write even when I'm sure I never will. And Anna, my daughter and friend, makes me laugh and keeps me grounded. They both provide endless support as I ask questions, pursue learning, and then write.

Why Learn with Multiple Sources?

1

*I*n a recent conversation with my seventh-grade daughter, she told me she was making plans to develop her own app. When I asked her how she planned to do this, she explained that she'd read several articles on the internet by app developers about how they got started. She told me that as she read, she realized most of the developers started by finding someone who knew more than they did, a mentor of sorts. One person had gone to a local university and found a technology student to help her get started; others had gone to local businesses and asked around. I had to smile. Weeks before, when Anna had first mentioned this endeavor, my husband and I had offered to find someone to help her get started, but she'd soundly rejected the idea. She had wanted to figure it out on her own. Reading multiple sources on this topic she cared about, though, had informed and transformed her thinking. Now she was embracing the idea of outside help.

What happened here? Anna had a question. She realized she didn't know enough about a topic that was important to her. She sought out multiple sources on the topic and deepened her understanding by synthesizing the information in those texts. Only then was she able to think critically about what she needed to do to move forward.

I asked Anna if she thinks kids do this naturally—read more than one text on a topic to answer their questions or deepen their understanding. She shrugged, unsure, and then said, "I think some kids might be like, 'I read this article and now I know what I'm talking about.'" When I asked Anna why she reads more than one text on a topic, she paused and then explained, "Well, I'm looking for different information, for more information I can add to my repertoire of what I already know. It's like when I was making muffins the other day. I looked at one recipe and saw a pretty good list of ingredients, but then I looked at another and it said to add cinnamon on top of the muffins. *Cinnamon on top!* That's the extra I'm looking for! Now I have an even better idea for making muffins."

This is what we want for our students. We want them to ask questions and then actively seek out answers by locating and reading or viewing multiple sources—articles, books, videos, photographs, infographics. We want them to think across those sources and be able to articulate for themselves as well as for others what they learned—orally and in writing. We also want them to *act* on what they learned—whether it's developing an app or making a better muffin or advocating for a particular issue or group.

Students are increasingly required to do this kind of thinking in school, as well. More and more, students are being asked to actively engage in thinking critically about multiple sources. This is a central focus in the *College, Career, and Civic Life (3C) Framework for Social Studies and Standards*, a guide released by the National Council for the Social Studies (2013, 6) to support states in developing new standards. The authors of this framework advocate strongly for teaching students to ask and answer their own questions and then seek out answers from multiple sources in order to be college, career, and civil life ready:

> *Now more than ever, students need the intellectual power to recognize societal problems; ask good questions and develop robust investigations into them; consider possible solutions and consequences; separate evidence-based claims from parochial opinions; and communicate and act upon what they learn. And most importantly, they must possess the capability and commitment to repeat that process as long as necessary. Young people need strong tools for, and methods of, clear and disciplined thinking in order to traverse successfully the worlds of college, career, and civic life.*

Students are also being asked to analyze and synthesize information from multiple sources on standardized tests. The questions and performance tasks on these assessments are rigorous, requiring students to think about many different aspects of a set of sources. Third-grade students have been asked to write an essay comparing and contrasting details in two articles. Fourth-grade students have been asked to integrate information from two sources—a text and a video clip—to write a report on a topic. Eighth-grade students have been asked to compare information in three sources—a video clip with four distinct segments and two passages including one with a diagram as a major feature. The texts are written in a variety of structures, including narrative, cause-effect, and problem-solution, and they reveal authors' points of view or are written from various perspectives, including the author's, an omnipotent narrator's, and even a person or animal's perspective while experiencing a particular event. The texts come from a diverse group of resources, including magazines like *Ranger Rick*, Scholastic's *SuperScience*, and Scholastic's *Storyworks*; youth-oriented websites like www.kidzworld.com; adult news sources like the *New York Times* and National Public Radio; and government websites like www.nasa.gov.

Like Anna, our students are also growing up with access to an endless amount of information—some of it fact and a lot of it opinion. Like many of the adults they know, the students receive "news" in short bites, skimming headlines or quickly reading synopses of an event. For many, their interpretation of what it means to be "informed" is skewed.

It is critical that we as educators teach students how to grapple with multiple sources on a topic or issue and that students have a chance to master doing this. A few years ago I realized that the instruction I offered students focused mainly on one source at a time and that I needed to make major changes in my practice. The students with whom my colleagues and I work need more opportunities to grapple with multiple sources on a topic or issue, and they need specific strategies for making sense of those sources. At first, I thought I knew what this would look like—I'd just use tricks of the trade like Venn diagrams and two-column notes. I'd start to talk more about what was "similar" and "different" between sources with students. I'd find cool sources to engage the students and we'd take off. But as I began to explore this further in real classrooms, I realized these tricks were primarily only good for a surface-level understanding of multiple sources. Nurturing a sense of being *informed* and *transformed* would require more instructionally.

With a group of colleagues—Nicole, Shannon, Micheline, Kelli, Meghan, Caleb, Kris, Martha, Karen, Chris, Anders, Emily, and Tara—and in my work with teachers across the country, I began to explore again. There were many lessons learned, and what has evolved is an approach to using multiple sources on a regular basis to teach. This book is about what we learned along the way.

What Does Reading Across Sources Look Like in a Classroom?

In a third-grade classroom, the students are seated on the carpet ready to take notes as they consult a third source on a topic. They are watching a video clip describing the Great Pacific Garbage Patch. They see images of trash that has been collected from the Pacific Ocean—bottle caps, tires, rubber shoes. They listen to a scientist describe the swollen bellies of fish that have ingested bits of plastic from the debris. Some of the students are quietly thinking, "Nothing new here. We've already read two articles about this." Then the narrator of the video states that the size of this floating field of garbage is twice the size of Texas. Suddenly, there's an audible gasp in the room. One student's hand flies up in the air. "Ms. Ballew! That deepens our knowledge!"

The students in that third-grade classroom were already familiar with the problem of ocean pollution because they had carefully consulted other sources on this topic. They'd analyzed a photograph of a loggerhead sea turtle being cared for at a sea turtle hospital and then closely read and annotated a related article about how many sea turtles munch on plastic debris. They had also read an informational text in the mandated anthology about how students pick up trash on California beaches once a year for Coastal Cleanup Day. So the students had some understanding of the problem—sea life is ingesting trash—and of one solution—humans are cleaning up the trash on beaches. Enough, right?

When I talked with the teacher, Nicole, about this later, she explained to me that despite engaging with these previous sources, the students still had no idea how big the problem of ocean pollution is until they watched the video and heard that fact comparing the size of the garbage patch to the size of Texas. With that simple comparison, their understanding of other details they'd read became clearer. Now statistics like "150 countries participate in Coastal Cleanup Day" and "112 million tons of debris is floating in garbage patches" in previous articles made more sense to these eight-year-olds. The images in the video of an endless amount of floating trash and the scientists' description of the weeks it took to navigate this field of debris helped the students create a clearer picture of the problem. More importantly, they realized that this problem is big and will not easily be solved by small groups of students picking up trash one day a year.

What Happens for Students as They Examine Multiple Sources?

Let's take a moment to think about how this kind of learning unfolds. In the book *Trapped! A Whale's Rescue* (Burleigh 2015), the author narrates the entrapment and rescue of a humpback caught in fishing nets off the coast of California in 2005. The author begins the book by describing the grace and beauty of this creature as she moves through the water, seeking food. "The huge humpback whale dips and dives. Her sleek black sides shimmering, she spyhops, lobtails, flashes her flukes" (2). Then the whale encounters the fishing nets.

Take a moment to read the excerpt in Figure 1.1 a–b. As you read, consider this question: What happens when the whale becomes entangled in the fisherman's net?

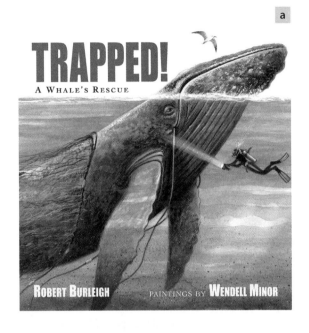

Figure 1.1 a–b Excerpt from *Trapped! A Whale's Rescue* (Burleigh 2015, 8–12)

But wait—danger haunts these waters.

Unseen nets, left by crab fishermen, drift through the dark sea.

The whale feels the tickle of thin threads. She plunges on. She tosses. She spirals sideways as spider lines tighten around her.

The struggle begins. The web of ropes cuts into her skin.

She flails, starts to sink, fights for air.

With each thrust of her tail, she tires.

Her sides heave. She flops. She flounders.

At last the great whale shudders and lies still.

In this short excerpt, Burleigh conveys the force of the ropes with phrases like "lines tighten" and "web of ropes cuts into her skin" and the futile struggle of the whale with phrases like "starts to sink," "tires," and "flounders." Burleigh's choice of words gives us a better understanding of what happened when the whale got tangled in the net. We also have a sense of the serious nature of this problem.

Now let's read an excerpt from an online news source, SFGate, about the same event in Figure 1.2. As you read, consider this question: How does this second source clarify your understanding of what happened to the whale?

In the first source, the excerpt from *Trapped! A Whale's Rescue* (Burleigh 2015), we learned the whale was entangled in a "web of ropes." In the second source, the news article, the author shares statistics or numerical facts about these ropes. There were a lot of ropes—"20." Each rope was "240 feet long," so the whale was trapped in thousands of feet of rope. The ropes were wrapped around the whale "at least four times." Attached to these ropes were "at least 12" crab traps that were heavy—"90 pounds each." These details clarify how the whale was pulled down, which would prevent it from breathing through its blowhole and, as a result, endanger its life. No wonder the whale was struggling: it was truly trapped, destined to die. Thinking carefully about the details in this second source in this way has clarified our understanding of what happened.

Next, we might consult a third source—a photograph and caption from www.worldwildlife.org that shows a diver attempting to free a sea turtle from a web of lines and nets so thick that it looks nearly like a mane of long, unruly hair. Only the turtle's front flippers and head protrude from the tangle. The caption, titled "The Problem of Bycatch," explains that billions of marine animals are accidentally caught and killed or mortally wounded each year. What can we add to the knowledge we developed by reading the first two sources?

Figure 1.2 Excerpt from "Daring Rescue of Whale off Farallones" (SFGate, Fimrite 2005)

About 20 crab-pot ropes, which are 240 feet long with weights every 60 feet, were wrapped around the animal. Rope was wrapped at least four times around the tail, the back and the left front flipper, and there was a line in the whale's mouth. . . . At least 12 crab traps, weighing 90 pounds each, hung off the whale, the divers said. The combined weight was pulling the whale downward.

After carefully thinking about each of these sources, we might want to know more. What can we do to help? Is there any hope? In another part of the www.worldwildlife.org site, there is an additional text about the International Smart Gear Competition, a competition hosted by the World Wildlife Foundation that challenges scientists and those in the fishing industry to find "smarter" ways to fish—ways that reduce bycatch.

The details in this source reveal an effect of or a response to the problem introduced in the first three sources. This source also provides new information to add to the knowledge we built when we looked carefully at the first three sources—there are groups trying to solve this problem.

What might happen for our students if they carefully thought about the information in these four sources? Chances are that their understanding of this topic would expand and deepen as they read each new source. How do they do this? They continually connect and clarify. As they read each new source, the students look for connections between the details in the different sources. How are the details similar? How are they different? How do they build on each other to help the reader form a fuller understanding of the topic? At the same time, the students are also clarifying their understanding. What confusions do they need to clear up? How does this all fit together? And what new questions do they have?

How Can We Help Students Read Across Sources?

Over the last few years, I've worked with colleagues across the country to develop a process for helping students read across sources with increasing independence. The major takeaways, each described in brief below, are at the heart of this book.

Establish Clear Purposes

Nonfiction texts can be dense with information. Students may become overwhelmed by so many details, or they may think they need to remember everything they have read or noticed in multiple sources. A purpose for reading stated as a question can make a huge difference. Notice how I provided you with a purpose for reading when I presented the first source—"What happens when the whale becomes entangled in the fisherman's net?" This question probably helped you determine what to pay attention to as you read and reread the excerpt. Questions like "How does weather affect people's lives?" and "After the American Revolution, how did political parties take shape?" can create clarity for students as they determine what is important to note in multiple sources. Initially, it may be up to us to develop these questions. Questions we develop for students also serve as models for the kinds of questions they can ask on their own later.

Chapter 2 provides some guidance on developing questions. Later, in Chapter 5, there are suggestions for how to teach your students to generate their own questions.

Develop Tight Sets of Sources

Have you ever asked students to compare two texts like a book and an article and received general responses like "They are both about Holocaust survivors" or "One author talked about friction and the other author talked about gravity"? It may be that there are too many details in these sources for students to hold on to cognitively and then also compare, contrast, and integrate—even with a clear guiding question. While there is a place for reading entire texts like the book *Trapped! A Whale's Rescue* (Burleigh 2015) or for viewing entire videos, comparing short sources like two excerpts of text or a one-minute video clip and a diagram can be just as cognitively demanding and is also *manageable*.

Chapter 2 includes suggestions for locating and identifying sources that are feasible for students to think across and for developing sets of sources that support each other like the four sources about bycatch that we examined earlier. Providing sources for students helps them begin to understand what relevant, truthful sources should look like when they do research on their own. Chapter 5 describes mini-lessons that help students identify relevant sources independently and vet those sources for credibility.

Teach Strategies

When we ask a question like "How is this source similar to or different from that one?" we are assessing what students understand. If they understand how two texts are the same or different, they may have an adequate response. If they do not, their response will be lacking. Questions like this do not teach students *how* to notice or recognize the similarities and differences in texts. A guiding question or purpose is a tool that students can use to examine the similarities and differences between two texts or to gather and integrate information from more than one source.

Chapter 3 includes nine lesson ideas that focus on teaching students about specific strategies or tools they can use for making sense of information in more than one source. These are designed to be adapted to your context for teaching. You can use these right away or you can integrate them into a larger unit of study. Chapter 5 also describes a key tool for helping students organize their thinking as they think strategically across sources—the inquiry chart.

Provide Support

As they tackle making sense of multiple sources, students need us to be present and ready to support them along the way. We may need to be think partners, ready to think aloud *for* and *with* students, letting students see and hear us make sense of a second and third source. They might be okay making sense of a video clip, but they might need us to step in and think aloud again when they confront a complex diagram. They may need us to use prompts during conferences that help them sustain a focus on the purpose for reading and help them use their notes from a first source to think about the information in a second source. They may need us to write *with* them in response to multiple sources, thinking aloud about how we reread our notes and then determined what to write.

Chapter 4 describes specific instructional moves we can use to move students forward in this endeavor. To be ready, we have to continually observe students, noticing what they are doing well and what they are struggling with and then stepping in to support at this point of need. In Chapter 5, there are examples of mini-lessons you can give when you notice particular obstacles to student learning.

Foster Independent Learning

Our ultimate goal is for students to ask their own questions, locate their own sources, and then independently and productively engage with multiple sources. This might be an open inquiry on a topic of their choice or as part of a mandated curriculum. This may happen at multiple points during an integrated unit of study.

As mentioned earlier, Chapter 5 includes advice on how to gradually release responsibility to students for generating questions, locating helpful sources, and grappling with the content in these sources. Chapter 6 offers suggestions for assessment to inform our instruction as we move students toward independence and to evaluate the sum of students' learning.

Teach with Multiple Sources Regularly

Traditionally, reading multiple informational texts on the same topic has been reserved for writing research reports, a big production that may occur only a few times a year.

Although doing major research projects is grand, reading multiple texts on the same topic a few times a year isn't enough practice for students to master the skills required to synthesize information from multiple sources. Students need *regular* opportunities to do this. This has been my biggest takeaway during my professional inquiry.

Chapter 7 describes how several of my colleagues who work in different school settings are integrating learning with multiple sources into their curriculum on a regular basis.

Planning: Establishing Purposes for Reading and Selecting Sources

2

What's your point of view on Christopher Columbus and his legacy? Was he courageous? Strategic? Arrogant? Cruel? During a unit of study on the early American explorers, my colleague Caleb asked his fifth-grade students to write their point of view regarding Christopher Columbus before they read, listened to, or viewed any sources. He posed the question, "What do you think about Christopher Columbus and his explorations in the New World? What is your point of view?" Many of the students quickly realized they did not know much about this historical figure. One student, Ashlan, wrote the following in her notes:

> Christopher Columbus was an explorer. He discovered
> America and was also very brave. I don't know much about
> him, but that is what I know.

Caleb continued the lesson by reading aloud two picture books, *Follow the Dream* (Sis 1991) and *Encounter* (Yolen 1992). Each of these books reveals a clear point of view. In *Follow the Dream*, a nonfiction account that follows Columbus as he plans his voyage, Sis reveals Columbus' strategic thinking and determination. In *Encounter*, Yolen shares a fictional perspective of one Taino youth who, after an ominous dream, is alarmed by the appearance of strangers on his community's shores and warns his people not to befriend Columbus and his crew. Caleb gave the students clear purposes for listening stated as questions:

- What is the author's point of view?
- What details in the text make you think so?
- How does this author's point of view influence your point of view?

After students listened to the books read aloud, they closely read short excerpts from these texts, underlined language that revealed each author's point of view, and wrote annotations. Then the teacher shared a third "text" or source—a video clip in which a narrator describes Columbus' three voyages. Included are details about how Columbus persuaded the royalty in Spain to fund his journey and how he enslaved the native peoples when he arrived after the second voyage. As they listened, the fifth-grade students took notes about the narrator's point of view. Then they engaged in student-led conversations comparing the different points of view in the three sources and examining how these influenced the students' points of view. When Ashlan wrote about how these sources influenced her point of view regarding Columbus, she stated:

> Some people say good things about Columbus and some people say bad things about Columbus. I have a fifty-fifty point of view because I think what he did was good and bad. I think he was greedy, but I also think he was brave and adventurous.

When we compare this description to Ashlan's original assessment of Columbus—that he was simply "very brave"—we can see how her perspective has become multidimensional. This is what we want for our students: the ability to look at multiple sources and triangulate meaning from a variety of perspectives.

Careful planning of purposes and selection of sources made this an effective learning experience for these students. As these fifth-grade students read or viewed each source, they had very clear purposes to guide them in determining importance. The teacher developed the purposes very intentionally with a clear objective. Keeping these questions as a focal point helped the students develop the skill of identifying author's point of view while also helping them learn content about the accomplishments of one explorer. The teacher was also intentional with the selection of sources—these three sources revealed contrasting points of view, making it easy for students to grasp the concept of author's point of view.

What Is a Purpose for Reading, and Why Does It Matter?

Have you ever conferred with students who struggle to determine what information is really important? A clearly stated purpose for reading multiple sources can make the difference between productive and unproductive reading and thinking for many students. A purpose, stated as a question like "What is the author's point of view?" or "How did the Jewish resistance members reveal their courage?" creates a clear pathway for determining what is important in a text. This also helps students say, "I need to pay attention to this information" or "This information doesn't help me think about my purpose, so I'm going to read on."

In the long run, we want students to develop their own reasons for reading. We want them to ask valuable questions that help them construct knowledge as they tackle multiple sources. But there is value in having teachers determine the purposes for reading, as well. There may be a skill we need to teach or specific content that is part of a mandated curriculum. Teacher-developed purposes are also strong examples of the kinds of questions students need to ask on their own. Chapter 5 provides models for releasing responsibility for learning to students, including teaching them how to ask their own questions and set purposes for reading. For now, let's explore teacher-developed purposes for reading.

A Purpose for Reading Might Be Focused on a Skill or on Content

"What is the author's point of view?" is a skill-focused purpose, and "What are essential components of an ecosystem?" and "How did members of the Jewish resistance act courageously?" are content-focused purposes. These two purposes—reading to become skillful and reading to learn content—work in service of each other. Figure 2.1 lists examples of both types of purposes. Each is stated as a question that students can easily ask themselves as they read, view, or listen to multiple sources on a topic.

Sample Skill-Focused Purposes (for addressing literacy goals)

Purposes related to main idea or central message:
- What is each author's main idea (or central message)?
- What details support each author's main idea(s)?
- How are the authors' main ideas similar and different?
- How are the most important points in these texts similar and different?

Purposes related to author's point of view or perspective:
- What is each author's point of view?
- What is your point of view? What details in the text influenced your point of view?
- What is each author's claim? How is that claim developed?
- How does each author develop credibility for a claim or point of view?

Purposes related to a text's structure:
- How does each author structure the presentation of the information?
- What are the differences and similarities in how these authors present the same event or information?
- How does each author introduce and elaborate on a particular idea? Event? Individual?

Sample Content-Focused Purposes (for addressing content-area goals)

Purposes related to units of study aligned with *Next Generation Science Standards* (NGSS Lead States 2013):

3rd grade	What happens to organisms when their environments change?
4th grade	What is energy and how is it related to motion?
5th grade	What is an example of a technology that was designed to solve a problem?
6th grade	What is the ocean's influence on weather and climate?

Purposes related to units of study aligned with the *College, Career, and Civic Life (C3) Framework for Social Studies State Standards* (NCSS 2013):

3rd grade	Who were the first people in my community?
4th grade	Why did different groups of people decide to settle in my state?
5th grade	What happened when Europeans encountered the indigenous peoples of America?
6th grade	How did the environment influence ancient ways of life?

Figure 2.1 Examples of Skill and Content-Focused Purposes for Reading

A Purpose for Reading Is Different from a Final Task or Project

The fifth-grade students described earlier might struggle if we simply said, "Your purpose for reading multiple texts is to write an article about an explorer." Many students might quickly become overwhelmed, thinking they have to remember everything they read in order to write the article. I remember visiting with two fifth-grade students who were planning to write a report on hedgehogs. They were so excited and one exclaimed, "We read a *whole* book about hedgehogs!" When I asked them what they learned that they would include in their report, they hesitated. Then one chirped, "We're going to write about the *whole* book!" While these students had a real sense of accomplishment, they did not have clarity about their purpose for reading or writing. They might have benefited from guiding questions like "What role does the hedgehog play in a healthy ecosystem?" and "How does the hedgehog's diet support its health?"

It is also important to note that reading or analyzing multiple sources in order to complete a final project does not have to always be the goal. If we are asking students to read across sources on a *regular basis*, they may do this just to inform short student-led conversations or brief written responses. For example, for a series of small-group lessons, a fourth-grade colleague paired two short texts that focus on how public officials accomplish tasks. One text was an article from the district-mandated McGraw-Hill *Wonders* anthology that described how public officials and committees run a town. The second source was an article on the internet about public officials' plans for alleviating high levels of lead in the municipal water supply in Flint, Michigan. Over the course of two twenty-minute lessons, with the teacher as a guide, the students read each text closely, talked with partners about what they were learning, and took notes. Then, in two additional twenty-minute lessons, they used the notes to write a draft of a letter to someone they thought should run for public office. Altogether, four short lessons were planned with a clear purpose for reading the two texts. This was not a big or long production, but a powerful approach nonetheless.

There May Be One Purpose or Multiple Purposes for Reading a Set of Sources

Whether there is one purpose or multiple purposes depends on the set of sources you are using and on your students. If a particular text in the set is complex, you may want to ask students to focus on only one purpose. If you are working with readers who need more support, you may want to provide only one purpose for reading. Or your students may read a complex text or set of texts multiple times—each time with a different purpose.

How Do We Develop Purposes for Reading Multiple Sources?

Developing clear purposes to guide students' reading or viewing or listening takes some planning on our part. What follows are some suggestions that might help.

Focus on the Content Your Students Need to Learn

Think about the social studies and science content you are teaching in the near future. How can this content be turned into questions or purposes for reading multiple sources? Later in the unit on American explorers, each of Caleb's students chose an explorer and read multiple sources on that historical figure. Caleb developed additional purposes to guide the students' research based on his district's curriculum: What were this explorer's goals? What did the explorer do to achieve these goals? What was the impact of this explorer's endeavors?

The themes or enduring understandings for a unit of study can also be turned into the purpose for reading multiple sources. Questions like "What is the role of engineering in the twenty-first century?" and "How might different kinds of knowledge contribute to the reduction of climate change and human vulnerability?" help students understand important ideas and can also guide their exploration of sources.

If there is a final project or task as part of a unit of study, what do students need to know to complete this endeavor? The "what" might become the purpose for reading. For example, if we are going to ask students to conduct an investigation to provide evidence that living things are made of cells, what do students need to know about cells before they can do this?

Use the Sets of Sources You Already Have

Many of us have much-loved sets of texts already. Read or view those sources again and think about which questions are answered in at least two of them. Turn these into your purposes for reading.

Some publishers provide purposes for reading or essential questions for texts in their anthologies. While some of these may be worthwhile, be cautious. Sometimes the publisher's questions are narrow and answered easily within a few sentences in the text. This doesn't provide much of a challenge for our readers. I've also found that sometimes the publisher's question is not answered at all or not answered very well in the text. Most importantly, the publisher doesn't have the knowledge you have about your students and about the curriculum you are required to teach.

Make Sure the Purposes Are Worthy of Students' Time

Strong purposes for reading or listening or viewing engage students in extracting important information or drawing conclusions from more than one source. Questions like "What were the obstacles the passengers faced when the *Titanic* began to sink?" or "How has weathering and erosion contributed to the formation of our state's landscape?" promote deeper thinking than a question like "What year did the *Titanic* sink?" While knowing the year the *Titanic* sank is helpful, students are not going to build depth of knowledge by reading multiple sources to answer this question. They should find this answer quickly and easily and then spend quality time with multiple sources contemplating higher-level thinking questions.

How Do We Locate Multiple Sources on the Same Topic?

The sources we choose need to help students respond to the purpose for reading. In other words, the sources need to provide content students can mull over as they respond to the questions we have posed. Students also need to engage with a variety of sources. As a result, up front, the task for selecting multiple sources may be ours. This can be a manageable task for us. Here are a few lessons I have learned.

Start with One or More Sources You Already Have

My first suggestion for putting together a set of sources is to start by locating one source on the topic that you like. This may be a source you already have. Read it or view it or listen to it again, and determine whether there is enough information related to the purpose you have developed to warrant a careful reading or analysis by your students. If there is, then use this as your first source and move on to locating additional texts. If there isn't, keep searching.

Typically, I do not use traditional science and social studies textbooks when engaging students in reading across texts. Frequently, there are too many facts or details and not enough elaboration on any of those details. For example, the description of a battle including who, what, when, where, and why is forced into three sentences. There's just not enough content worthy of students' consideration, especially if they are thinking through responses to higher-level questions. An exception to this rule is that you may choose to begin with an excerpt from a traditional textbook and then locate a richer source on the same topic. For example, for a sixth-grade lesson on the life of Spartan soldiers in ancient Greece, I started with the following paragraph from the textbook *Reflections: Ancient Civilizations* (Harcourt School Publishers 2007, 298). This was the only description of the young Spartans in this text. Notice how the author's language makes the young Spartans' life seem decent and manageable:

> *From an early age, Spartans learned to be strong and disciplined. At the age of seven, boys were sent to live in training camps to get a Spartan education. At the training camps, boys lived and ate together in barracks. Every day, they practiced gymnastics, wrestling, and military exercises. They learned to accept hardship without complaint and to obey orders without question.*

Then I added a text from www.history.com titled "8 Reasons It Wasn't Easy Being Spartan" (Andrews 2013). I located this text by searching on the internet with the key words "Spartan soldier training." This is a short excerpt from a longer text I used with students. Notice the difference in the author's perspective:

> *At the age of 7, Spartan boys were removed from their parents' homes and began the "agoge," a state-sponsored training regimen designed to mold them into skilled warriors and moral citizens. Separated from their families and housed in communal barracks, the young soldiers-in-waiting were instructed in scholastics, warfare, stealth, hunting and athletics. At age 12, initiates were deprived of all clothing save for a red cloak and forced to sleep outside and make their own beds from reeds. To ready them for a life in the field, the boy soldiers were also encouraged to scavenge and even steal their food, though if detected they were punished with floggings.*

This second text serves to support and extend the information in the first text. There are details that are the same, but there are also new details that provide a different perspective on the experiences of the Spartans. If you are going to use excerpts from a textbook, then consider adding texts that can enrich conversations and written responses.

Choose a Variety of Sources

Sources come in many shapes and sizes. Consider diverse formats (e.g., articles, photographs, infographics, or videos) in a mix of genres (e.g., narrative, explanatory, descriptive, persuasive, or argumentative). Think about primary sources as well as secondary sources. The use of different formats helps authors shape the same information in different ways. As a result, diverse sets of sources promote critical thinking.

Go for Shorter Sources

It's fine to select one paragraph or a few pages as a source. You can also identify thirty seconds of a video clip or one diagram as a source. If a source is manageable, students are more likely to recall specific details and, as a result, can more easily compare and contrast those details with new information as they examine additional sources. When Nicole, a third-grade teacher, and I began planning a unit of study on simple machines for her class, we quickly realized that the texts were dense with difficult facts that would be hard to remember if the texts were too long. Consider the following excerpt about the wedge from *Simple Machines: Wheels, Levers, and Pulleys* (Adler 2015, 2):

> *A wedge is thin at one end and wide at the other. It's a simple machine that helps break things apart.*
>
> *Your teeth are wedges. When you bite into an apple, the sharp, thin end of your teeth split the apple.*

There are a lot of details to remember in just four sentences. In the first sentence, Adler describes the physical attributes of the wedge—"thin at one end and wide at the other." Then he tells the reader the purpose of the wedge—"helps breaks things apart." Next he moves on to give an example of a wedge—"your teeth'"—and explain how your teeth act as a wedge—"When you bite into an apple, the sharp, thin end of your teeth split the apple." In the book, Adler goes on to describe three more real-life examples of wedges and then to explain and give examples of five more simple machines. For this particular unit, the teacher and I ended up choosing a few short excerpts from multiple texts about each simple machine for students to read and compare.

For a second text on wedges, we chose the following from *Machines Make It Move* (Tomecek 2003, 8):

> *Wedges come in two basic varieties: broad and flat like the head of an ax, or round and pointed like the tip of an arrow. Early humans probably didn't invent wedges but used naturally pointy sticks and stones. Eventually people learned how to make the wedges by shaping rocks and sticks. They were even able to make knives as sharp as most modern day blades.*

This text is dense in details, too. Just in the first sentence, Tomecek, the author, describes two different types of wedges and compares them to other objects. Then he goes into a brief explanation of the history of how wedges may have evolved. We chose the second text because it supports the information in the first text and extends it as well. Students can add descriptive details like "broad and flat" to details they read in the first text like "thin at one end and wide at the other." They can extend their understanding by adding additional real-life examples—"like the head of an ax" and "like the tip of an arrow"—to the one they learned about in the first text—"teeth." And so forth.

"Short and manageable" goes for video clips and audio files, too. My colleague Kelli and I were teaching fifth-grade students to tackle multiple sources as part of a unit of study on ecosystems. When I started hunting for a relevant video clip, I quickly became overwhelmed by how much information can be crammed visually and auditorily into just a few seconds. We ended up using less than thirty seconds of a video as a source, and even then the students needed to watch it twice to begin to identify relevant details and then again to be able to understand those details. I remember at one point the students were so busy listening for important details that I had to remind them to *also watch* the video because there was an important graphic to consider.

Build a Set of Sources That Support Each Other

As you begin to develop a set of sources, think about how the information provided in each source supports and/or extends the information in the other sources. As with the two texts about the wedge, I try to layer sources so that when students read a second, third, or fourth text, they start to notice details that are the same or they begin to notice information that is different and that can be added to what they learned in a previous text. For example, Kelli and I chose two diagrams to use at the beginning of that fifth-grade unit on ecosystems. The first diagram was a simple illustration with basic terms like *producer*, *consumer*, and *decomposer*. The arrows in the diagram supported the reader in inferring processes like "some animals eat plants" and "some animals eat other animals." The second diagram was more complex, with more difficult terms like *primary consumers* and *secondary consumers* and detailed captions that explained how processes like decomposition occur. When we posted the second diagram for the students to observe, there was an audible gasp in the room. The students immediately recognized that the diagram was illustrating how an ecosystem works. This made it much easier for them to dig in and think about the more difficult concepts presented.

A team of educators in the Chicago Public Schools (CPS) and I developed a unit of study for third-grade students focused on Jim Crow laws in the South and the work of civil rights activists during the 1950s and 1960s. The unit included reading aloud several books to students and also asking them to closely read or analyze text excerpts from those books and numerous other sources in order to write and talk in response. The three sources in Figures 2.2 through 2.4 were chosen to help students develop an understanding of the laws' injustice. Notice how the second and third sources extend students' understanding of the laws described in the first source. Vocabulary like *indignity* and *dignity* can easily be used to discuss all three texts.

Examples of Text Set for Third-Grade Unit of Study on Civil Rights

My brothers and I grew up a long time ago. Back in a time when certain places in our country had unfair laws that said it was right to keep black people separate because our skin was darker. . . .

Atlanta, Georgia, the city in which we were growing up, had those laws. Because of those laws, my family rarely went to the picture shows or visited Grant Park with its famous Cyclorama. In fact, to this very day I don't recall ever seeing my father on a streetcar. Because of those laws, and the indignity that went with them, Daddy preferred keeping M.A., A.D., and me close to home, where we'd be protected.

Figure 2.2 Excerpt from *My Brother Martin: A Sister Remembers Growing Up with the Rev. Dr. Martin Luther King Jr.* (Farris 2003, 9–12)

SOURCE 1

SOURCE 2

Figure 2.3 Photo of Segregated Water Cooler in
Oklahoma City, Oklahoma (Lee 1939)

On one shopping trip, the saleswoman would not serve them until after all the white customers had been helped. Westley had heard the saleswoman politely call the white women customers "Miss" and "Mrs." But she treated his grandma as if she were a child, a nobody. Westley's grandma pretended not to notice. She was polite. But she was also proud. "Come on," she said, "it's time to go home." They left the store without buying a thing.

SOURCE 3

Figure 2.4 Excerpt from *Delivering Justice: W. W. Law and the Fight for Civil Rights* (Haskins 2005, 4)

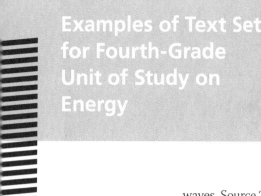

A colleague and I planned a unit of study on energy aligned with the Next Generation Science Standards. We started by developing a set of sources that could help students answer the question, "How does sound travel?" We selected the four sources in Figures 2.5 through 2.8 to use with students. Students had the opportunity to read each article a few times before closely reading the excerpt. Students also had an opportunity to think aloud about the diagrams in small groups.

As you read, notice how the diagram of the sound waves, Source 2, illustrates the information in the first and second paragraphs of Source 1. Source 3 is clear enough that students could work on their own to figure out the progression of sound through the ear and to the brain. Source 4 extends the students' learning with information about how sound also travels by bone conduction.

Figure 2.5
Excerpt from "Can You Ride a Sound Wave?" from Wonderopolis (2017)

Sound waves move through the air around you most of the time. While the air might seem rather empty, it's actually filled with lots of air molecules. When vibrating objects, such as your vocal cords or the strings of a piano, make sounds, they do so by causing the air molecules to move in waves that your ears receive and interpret as sounds.

Sound needs air molecules to travel. That's why no one would be able to hear you if you screamed in outer space. The absence of air—called a vacuum—in outer space prevents sound from traveling.

You've probably seen a lot of science-fiction movies that feature spectacular battles in outer space. Lasers flash across the sky and spaceships explode in loud bursts of sound and light. In reality, you'd be able to see, but not hear, those explosions. Moviemakers add sound to make the experience of watching the movie better.

Here on Earth, though, there are plenty of air molecules to help sound travel. In fact, sound travels really fast through the air. How fast? Sound moves at a quick 1,125 feet per second in dry air at 68° F at sea level. That's about 767 miles per hour or approximately a mile in five seconds!

SOURCE 1

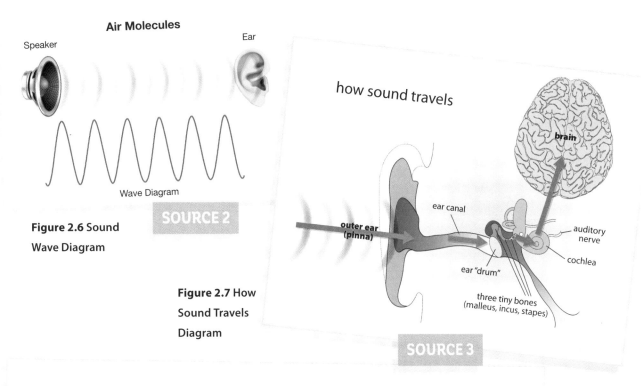

Air Molecules

Speaker

Ear

Wave Diagram

Figure 2.6 Sound Wave Diagram

SOURCE 2

how sound travels

brain

ear canal

outer ear (pinna)

auditory nerve

cochlea

ear "drum"

three tiny bones (malleus, incus, stapes)

Figure 2.7 How Sound Travels Diagram

SOURCE 3

The ear's hearing mechanisms lie deep within the inner ear. Sound reaches the inner ear in a couple of different ways. Most of what we hear is the result of air conduction. Things that make sounds cause sound waves that are transmitted through the air.

Those sound waves reach your outer ear and travel through the eardrum and middle ear to the cochlea, which is the fluid-filled spiral organ in the inner ear that translates those waves to the brain. Through the air isn't the only way sounds reach the inner ear, though. The bones and tissues inside your head can also conduct sound waves directly to the cochlea.

When you speak, your vocal cords create sound waves that travel through the air to reach your inner ear. The bones and tissues in your head, however, also conduct those sound waves directly to your cochlea, so that the voice you hear in your head when you speak is the result of both methods of transmission.

When you hear your voice on a recording, you're only hearing sounds transmitted via air conduction. Since you're missing the part of the sound that comes from bone conduction within the head, your voice sounds different to you on a recording.

Figure 2.8 Excerpt from "Why Does My Voice Sound Different on a Recording?" from Wonderopolis (2017)

SOURCE 4

Be Wary of Pre-paired Texts

Some current publishers' textbooks include "paired texts." These might work, but be cautious. Some texts may not work together as well as the publisher planned. For example, one of the McGraw-Hill *Wonders* third-grade leveled texts is about the astronaut Dr. Franklin Chang-Díaz, who overcame many challenges as a youth and adult to qualify for NASA's astronaut program. The text lends itself to thinking critically about how Chang-Díaz set goals and persevered to achieve those goals. The paired text is a fictional account of a girl named Melina who overcomes two obstacles to become an astronaut. Unfortunately, the author describes Melina's obstacles in two sentences without any elaboration and does not explain *how* she overcame those obstacles. The rest of the short three-page story describes what she did as an astronaut. There's just not enough content in this second text for students to contrast with that of the first. When the team of teachers with whom I was planning noticed this issue, they quickly got on the internet and located a different text to pair with the book about Chang-Díaz—a short video describing the obstacles the astronaut Mae Jemison faced.

Make Building Sets of Sources Manageable

There are a lot of sources out there. When I first started building sets of sources with my colleague Nicole, we quickly became overwhelmed by how many sources we might share with students. We had to make it manageable for ourselves. So we set parameters—for each set of sources we found the following:

- one short text or excerpt from a longer text
- one graphic (e.g., diagram, graph, map)
- one video clip.

As we created these sets, we started relying on particular resources or places to find sources. Eventually, with practice, we could find sources more quickly and create larger sets of sources as a result.

As you search for texts, find resources that you can return to continually—resources that are aligned with the curriculum and are consistently well written. In Figure 2.9, I have included several of my "go-to" internet sites. I also hit the library and pull every book on a particular topic off the shelf. Then I sit down and flip through each, hunting for relevant short passages, images, or infographics. I have favorite nonfiction authors, too. If I'm going to be selecting texts about simple machines, I know I'm going to look for a book by Sally M. Walker. If I I'm looking for a text on a particular event in history, I look to see if Candace Fleming or Steve Sheinkin have written about it. Over time, I've archived links to sources in Word documents and on my bookshelf so I can use them again and again.

"Go-To" Internet Resources for Texts

There are so many resources on the Internet. Frequently, I will just do a general search on a topic and add "for kids" to my search term—for example, "plate tectonics for kids." I also click on the "images" tab after I've done a search in order to see what kinds of photographs, illustrations, or infographics are available. Figure 2.9 lists sites that I frequent because of the consistency in quality of writing.

Figure 2.9 "Go-To" Internet Resources for Texts

Website Name	URL	Description
Wonderopolis	http://wonderopolis.org	This site has science-related articles on high-interest topics. Articles continually encourage readers to ask their own questions.
Newsela	https://newsela.com	The developers at this site have adapted current events articles from publications like the *Washington Post* and the *Orange County Register* to provide multiple versions on different readability levels. I find the articles at higher readability levels to be the most well written.
Science News for Students	https://student.societyforscience.org/sciencenews-students	The authors address current science topics and frequently include descriptions of specific research studies. I'd recommend this for savvy fifth- or sixth-grade readers. It's a good resource when you want students to analyze how authors writing about the same topic shape their presentation of the information differently.
Scholastic News	http://magazines.scholastic.com	Scholastic News has archived previous articles from its magazine.
History	www.history.com	This site has articles, short videos, and photographs of primary sources on a wide variety of topics.
Biography	www.biography.com	This site provides information about most historical figures. It consistently includes short articles and videos on each person.
National Aeronautics and Space Administration	www.nasa.gov	NASA's site offers articles and features (photographs, diagrams, etc.) on numerous science topics related to aeronautics and space.

Developing a Clear Purpose and Creating a Source Set Take Time

Traditionally, reading multiple sources on a topic has been reserved for major research projects, and it's possible that we only had to think about assembling sets of sources a few times a year. It's a big move to do this on a regular basis. Make this manageable for yourself by taking small steps. I mentioned that Nicole and I set parameters on how many and what types of sources we would collect. Some teams of teachers divvy up topics as a way to divide and conquer the development of source sets.

The value of this endeavor becomes clear when you see your students' eyes light up as they examine a second, third, and fourth source on a topic. Students begin to see patterns in the information they are learning, and they begin to recognize how information from a previous source is useful in understanding the next source. They can talk for longer about a topic and have more to say when they write. Over time, students develop a sense of agency. They say to themselves, "I can tackle multiple sources on a topic!" and they begin to see how they can read their way to becoming experts. This is what we want for students—strong identities as strategic readers, writers, thinkers. Many students even become addicted to reading multiple sources on the same topic. In Nicole's classroom, her students have started asking on a regular basis, "Can we find *another* source about this, too?"

Teaching: Lesson Ideas for Reading and Thinking Across Sources

3

We need a variety of sources so we get the whole story.

We need to understand all the points of view that could be related to the topic.

We need to gather as many facts as we can until we meaningfully understand.

It's important to see videos and pictures too—not just text— because we can hear and see emotion and their voice to really understand how they were feeling.

—FOURTH-GRADE STUDENTS

As part of a unit of study on the civil rights movement, these students tackled essential questions like "What were segregated schools like?" and "Why were segregated schools a violation of civil rights?" The students explored a variety of texts. They read and annotated excerpts from *Separate Is Never Equal: Sylvia Mendez & Her Family's Fight for Desegregation* (Tonatiuh 2014) and *Heroes for Civil Rights* (Adler 2008) and examined primary sources, including photos that revealed the difference between schools for colored students and schools for white students. They also listened to audio files of African American and Mexican American individuals recounting their experiences as young people attempting to integrate all-white schools.

The essential questions served as the purposes for reading and as a guide for determining what was important when taking notes. The teacher modeled what this looked like by thinking aloud in front of the students and modeled writing her own notes. Ultimately the students wrote essays from the perspective of a child or teenager who was part of this complex period in history.

As revealed in the comments that open this chapter, there is a lot of potential for learning when students read multiple texts. The possibilities expand, though, if our selection of those texts and instruction with those texts is focused and purposeful.

▌ How to Get Started

What follows are lesson ideas for helping students understand the information in two or more sources. First, Figure 3.1 provides a brief description of each lesson, the types of nonfiction texts that would work with each lesson, and when to use that lesson. A bit later in the chapter, detailed descriptions of each lesson are provided, including sample sources that you may be able to locate easily on the internet or at the library for an initial lesson, if appropriate for your students. Also notice that each lesson includes a purpose for reading stated as a question. In my experience, each of these lessons needs to be used multiple times with several pairs or sets of sources so students have a chance to master the strategies involved.

Ideally, these lessons would also be part of a content area or integrated unit of study. The more background knowledge students bring to a text, the better they will understand it. If they are engaged in content-area hands-on learning or inquiry on the same topic as the texts, comprehending those texts will be easier. If this is not an option, the following lesson ideas could also be developed into a short series of reading lessons outside a unit of study. Or these ideas may simply serve as seeds for developing other types of lessons. Use these ideas as a way to grow your own.

Terminology

- **Source or text:** any material that can be examined carefully for the purposes of learning, including excerpts from books, photographs, maps, diagrams, and video or audio clips

- **Narrative text:** a type of nonfiction that recounts or tells the story of an event or experience

- **Informational or nonnarrative text:** a type of nonfiction with the primary goal of informing the reader about the natural or social world

- **Text features:** elements of a text that help a reader navigate a text (e.g., table of contents and headings) or that provide additional content to support or develop an idea in the text (e.g., photographs and captions, maps, diagrams)

- **Infographic:** a visual image like a diagram, chart, table, or graph that represents some sort of information or data

- **Primary sources:** raw materials or artifacts created during a specific time period (photographs, government documents, diary entries, etc.) or later in the form of eyewitnesses' or participants' accounts or reflections (memoirs, oral histories, etc.)

Figure 3.1 The Lesson Ideas and When to Use Them

Lesson Idea	Strategy	Type of Source	Use This When . . .
1. **Realize the Value of Reading More Than One Source on a Topic**	Students ask the question, "What did we just add to our learning?" as they read each additional source.	Two to three sources (infographics, video clips, text excerpts) on a high-interest topic	Your students are new to thinking carefully about multiple sources on a topic, or they need to review what happens for learners when they consult multiple sources on a topic.
2. **Make Connections Between a Feature and a Short Text**	Students annotate side-by-side sources and draw arrows between connecting details.	Short nonnarrative or narrative text and feature (e.g., map, diagram, photo, caption)	Students need to learn how to closely examine the details in text features and how those details support the information in another source.
3. **Be THIEVES to Make Informed Predictions**	Students use the THIEVES mnemonic (adapted from Manz 2002).	Two texts with multiple features (e.g., title, subheadings, visuals) that can be previewed before reading	Students need to work on making predictions about what they will learn from a source based on what they have learned from previous sources.

(continues)

Figure 3.1 The Lesson Ideas and When to Use Them (*continued*)

Lesson Idea	Strategy	Type of Source	Use This When . . .
4. Use the Coding Method to Self-Monitor and Compare	Students pause to ask questions about what they just read like "Is this new information?" or "Did I already read this in another source?" or "Do I understand this?" Then they "code" their thinking while annotating the source (adapted from Hoyt 2008).	Two or more sources on a topic	Students need a strategy to help them think about their thinking as they read or view multiple sources.
5. Name the Types of Details to Compare	Students compare information presented in multiple texts on the same topic by identifying the types of details authors use to describe or explain.	Two or more short nonnarrative texts (or excerpts) that describe something or explain how something works or occurs	Students need help recalling and comparing specific details they read in more than one source. This strategy can be particularly helpful when teaching students to read science texts.
6. Sketch a Combination of Details to Integrate	Students combine details from two or more texts on a topic to sketch a quick illustration.	Two or more short nonnarrative (often science-related) texts or excerpts that describe something or explain how something works or occurs	Students need help integrating details from more than one source.
7. Use a Thematic or Main Idea Question as a Guide	Students use a big question like "How was this person *innovative*?"	Two or more sources (primary or secondary) that narrate or provide information about the experiences of individual figures or groups (including short video clips)	Students need help thinking about big ideas with supporting details that are revealed across sources.
8. Examine Texts That Have Different Purposes	Students identify authors' differing purposes.	Two or more sources (text excerpts, video clips, infographics) on the same topic or issue but with different purposes (including primary sources)	Students need to develop a fuller picture of the topic.
9. Compare the Texts' Structures	Students analyze texts' structures.	Two or more texts on the same topic or issue, but with different structures	Students need support in navigating texts and owning the information in the texts.

A Note About Reading Comprehension Standards

If you're required to meet particular reading comprehension standards, you're in luck. The lessons in this chapter are packed with skills that are common in standards. Are we teaching students to *compare and contrast details*? To *integrate details*? To *analyze* how *two or more authors* write about a particular topic? All of the above! Readers naturally use all these skills any time they think about two or more texts, and in these lessons students engage in these skills as well. For example, in Lesson Idea 2: Make Connections Between a Feature and a Short Text, readers compare information in a text with information in a text feature, and then they integrate information they learned from both.

Suggestions for Efficient Text Introductions

All the lessons that follow involve introducing the text to students. Introducing non-fiction texts can take up a lot of valuable time, leaving less time for students to read and think strategically. At the same time, a good introduction is vital to supporting students' understanding when they go to read that text. Below are a few suggestions for introducing texts. You might implement two or more during a single introduction.

- Provide a one- to two-sentence gist statement about one or both sources. If appropriate, include information that answers these questions: What are these sources mostly about? How will the sources help the students understand the essential question better?

- Review the essential question(s) or purposes for reading relevant to these sources.

- Ask the students to briefly preview the sources and then make informed predictions.

- Teach a vocabulary word like *innovative*, *courageous*, or *perseverant* that is part of the essential question and that will be helpful in understanding the text. Try following these four quick steps when you introduce a new word:

  1. Before the lesson, write a kid-friendly definition on chart paper. During the lesson, state the definition and post it for all students to view. A kid-friendly definition of *innovative* is "tending to introduce something new or different, including a method or a way of doing something or an invention."

2. Make a connection to your own life with a sentence like "I was innovative when . . ."

3. Ask partners to make connections to their lives, using the word in their explanation. If needed, provide a stem like "I was innovative when . . ."

4. Briefly connect the word to the text the students will be reading. You could say, "In these texts, you will be reading about scientists who are innovative. That means in some way these scientists have introduced something new or different."

Lesson Idea 1

Realize the Value of Reading More Than One Source on a Topic

TYPE OF SOURCE
Two to three sources (infographics, video clips, text excerpts) on a high-interest topic

TIME
Two 40-minute lessons

STRATEGY
Students ask the question, "What did we just add to our learning?" and begin to realize the value of analyzing more than one source on a topic.

1

GETTING READY

1. **Select sources:** Choose an appropriate high-interest topic and locate two or three related sources. The sources you read in Chapter 1 (listed below) are on a topic that might easily engage students.

   • *Trapped! A Whale's Rescue* (Burleigh 2015)

   • SFGate article "Daring Rescue of Whale off Farallones" (Fimrite 2005)

   • Additional sources like a photograph of an entrapped sea turtle or information at www.wildlife.org about the International Smart Gear Competition

2. **Study the sources:**

   • Is there a short section in each text that is worth reading closely to compare details?

   • Does one text include a detail that the other did not? How does that detail add to the reader's learning about the topic?

   • What question about the topic might you ask that would help the students see the similarities and differences in these sources? For example, for the whale texts, the question might be *What did you learn about the entrapment of sea creatures in fishing nets?*

3. **Prepare materials:** Determine how students will view the sources. You might read a book aloud, give the students hard copies of excerpts or articles, and project photographs or video clips.

BEGINNING THE LESSON

Today we are going to think about why it is helpful to read more than one text or source on a topic. We are going to read or look closely at three, asking ourselves after each one, "What did we just add to our learning?"

Introduce the first text. For *Trapped! A Whale's Rescue*, you might say, *This book is a narrative about one whale who was caught in a fishing net off the coast of California in 2005. The whale became entrapped, which means she was caught and unable to escape on her own. While I'm reading this aloud, think about this question: What are you learning about the entrapment of sea creatures in fishing nets?*

Read the text aloud or ask students to read, and then discuss their responses before moving on to closely reading the excerpt from this text.

Teaching with Source 1

Let's closely read an excerpt or section of this text and think about what we are learning about this topic. (Pause to give the students time to read the excerpt.) *What are important words or phrases that we want to remember or that help us answer our question?*

Model underlining a phrase and jotting your thinking in the margins of the text. With the excerpt from *Trapped!* in Figure 3.2, you might say, *When I saw the words "spider lines tighten around her," I realized that the lines are getting tighter, and they are not going to be easy to get out of. This helps me answer the question, "What did I learn about the sea creature's entrapment?" I'm going to underline this phrase and jot down what I'm thinking.*

Encourage the students to continue annotating the text with a partner or on their own. Lean in to partner conversations and prompt them to share their thinking.

Figure 3.2 Excerpt from *Trapped! A Whale's Rescue* (Burleigh 2015, 8–12) with example of an annotation

But wait—danger haunts these waters.

Unseen nets, left by crab fishermen, drift through the dark sea.

The whale feels the tickle of thin threads. She plunges on. She tosses. She spirals sideways as spider lines tighten around her.

The lines are getting tighter, which might make it harder to escape!

The struggle begins. The web of ropes cuts into her skin.

She flails, starts to sink, fights for air.

With each thrust of her tail, she tires.

Her sides heave. She flops. She flounders.

At last the great whale shudders and lies still.

SOURCE 1

Teaching with Source 2

Briefly introduce the second text. Ask the students to read the whole text before engaging in closely reading the excerpt. When they begin to closely read the excerpt of the second text or source, ask them to consider the question, "What are you adding to your learning?" Post this question for all students to see, and pose this question as you confer with individuals or small groups.

Also be prepared to think aloud again about what you might underline and write in the margins. For example, with the second source on the whale being trapped in Figure 3.3, you might say, *In this first sentence—"About 20 crab-pot ropes, which are 240 feet long with weights every 60 feet, were wrapped around the animal"—the author tells me how many ropes there were—20—and how long they were—240 feet. That is a lot of rope and they were heavy, too! I'm going to underline those details and jot my thinking in the margins. This adds to my learning about the whale's entrapment, but it also really helps me better understand the gravity of this situation for the whale. What other details jump out at you and add to your learning?*

Figure 3.3 Excerpt from "Daring Rescue of Whale off Farallones" (SFGate, Fimrite 2005) with example of an annotation

About 20 crab-pot ropes, which are 240 feet long with weights every 60 feet, were wrapped around the animal. Rope was wrapped at least four times around the tail, the back and the left front flipper, and there was a line in the whale's mouth. . . . At least 12 crab traps, weighing 90 pounds each, hung off the whale, the divers said. The combined weight was pulling the whale downward.

Knowing how many and how long helps me picture in my mind how dangerous this was for the whale. That is a lot of rope to escape from!

SOURCE 2

Teaching with Additional Sources on This Topic

Implement a similar routine of briefly introducing sources and then asking students to consider the question, "What are you adding to your learning?" as they mark the texts or view or listen to other sources and jot their thinking. Be prepared to think aloud for the group or as you meet with individuals.

With the sources about trapped sea creatures, the third source might be a photograph of a sea turtle or other creature trapped in a net. For me, this broadens our understanding of the first two sources. If I thought aloud for students, I might say, *This source makes me realize that it's not just whales in trouble. There are other sea creatures affected by fishing nets.* I might prompt the students to look closely at the photo, drawing conclusions about the turtle's entrapment and about the young man's intentions as he holds the knife to the net.

Provide time for the students to talk in small groups about the similarities and differences between the sources. Lean in to listen and confer. Close with questions like

- *Why was it important to read more than one source on this topic?*

- *How did you add to or change your understanding each time you read a new source?*

Questions to Push Kids' Thinking

- *What information did you add to your learning when you read this other text?*

- *What does that make you think? How can you jot that in a few words in the margin of the text?*

- *What would you have missed learning from this text if you had only read the first text?*

- If applicable, you might refer back to the essential question posed for students to consider as they read and ask, *How does this help you answer our question?*

Finding the Right Sources

- When looking for hot topics, you might search on news sites like www.usatoday.com. Once you find an article, search on the internet for additional sources on that topic.

- You might think about hot topics related to sports or high-profile figures. Given the recent national anthem protests by NFL teams, students might find engaging a lesson comparing the details in articles about these protests to those about protests by athletes in the more distant past.

- Keep in mind the creator or developer of the sources you choose and their purpose. Sometimes "hot topic" websites like BuzzFeed are meant more for entertainment than for learning facts and as a result are not as reliable. In later lessons, you can explore this issue further. For this lesson, though, you can help students consider sources by casually posing questions during the lesson to initiate students' awareness like "What do you think the author's purpose was in writing this text?"

Lesson Idea 2

Make Connections Between a Feature and a Short Text

TYPE OF SOURCE	TIME	STRATEGY
Short nonnarrative or narrative text and feature (e.g., map, diagram, photo, caption)	One 40-minute lesson	Students annotate side-by-side sources and draw arrows between connecting details.

GETTING READY

1. **Select sources:** Choose a text and a feature like a photograph, map, or diagram whose details are similar to those in the text or expand the ideas in the text. An easy way to start is to choose sources from the same book. For the lesson described below, the teacher chose an excerpt of text and photograph with a caption that were from the same book.

2. **Study the sources:**

   • Is there a purpose for reading stated as a question that can be answered with the text and feature you've chosen? (For the texts below, we used one of the essential questions from our unit of study: *How did the Native Americans use natural resources in their daily lives?*)

   • What details connecting the text and the feature do you want your students to notice?

   • What two details—one in the text and one in the feature— might you think aloud about in front of students?

3. **Prepare materials:** Provide a hard copy of the text and the feature on the same page or on two pages the students can place side by side. (When you repeat this lesson later with fresh texts, students can simply view the texts and write details in their notes, drawing arrows between the details to make connections.)

BEGINNING THE LESSON

What we learn from text features like maps, diagrams, and photographs can help us better understand texts that have just words in sentences and paragraphs. We do this by looking carefully at the text feature and making notes about what we are learning about the topic. Then when we read the text, we keep in mind what we learned from the feature and make connections to the text.

Introduce the feature and text briefly as well as the purpose for reading. For example, with the photograph and text below about the Algonquin people, you might say, *This is a feature and short text that will help us answer one of the big questions in our unit: "How did the Native Americans use natural resources in their daily lives?"* Provide time for the students to look at both before continuing.

Teaching with Source 1

Let's slow down and look at this feature before we read the text. I am going to start by asking myself, "What are details in this feature that I can learn about my topic?" Then I am going to jot notes in the margins about what I learned.

Think aloud for the students. With the photograph in Figure 3.4, you might say, *I read the caption and learned that this is a photo of a wigwam. When I looked at the picture, I noticed that it looks like there is tree bark on the outside of the wigwam. The pieces of bark or wood are bent toward the center. I'm going to draw an arrow from the bark to the margins and jot a note about this that says, "Some kind of wood bent toward center."* (Refer back to the essential question.) *Now I'm beginning to understand how the Algonquin tribe used natural resources in their daily lives.*

Ask the students to continue looking carefully and to write notes about what they see. Prompt partners to share: *Turn and talk with a partner. What did you notice? What did you decide to write?*

Figure 3.4
Excerpt from
Algonquin **(Tieck 2015, 9) with examples of annotations**

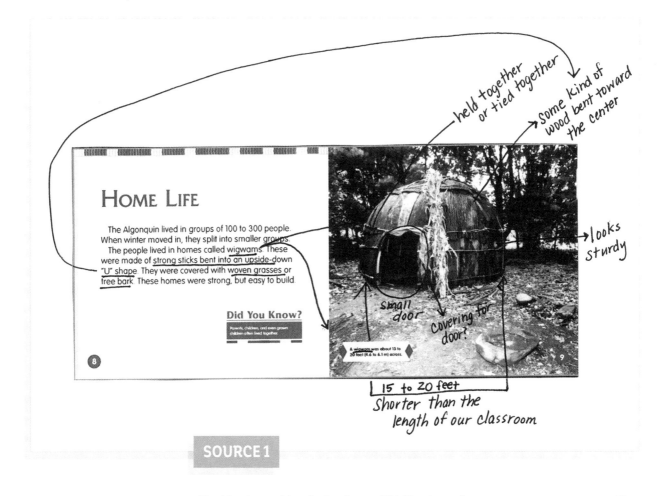

Teaching with Source 2

With the text in Figure 3.4, you might say, *Now I am going to think about what I am learning while I read the second source. As I read and write notes about what I'm learning, I'm going to make connections between what I learned in the photograph and caption and what I learned in the text or the words. I'm going to draw arrows from the feature to the text when I make a connection.*

Provide time for students to read and reread the whole text. Then, if needed, think aloud for the students about a connection between a detail in the text and a detail in the photograph. For example, *When I read, "The people lived in homes called wigwams," I knew what that looked like because I had seen the photograph. I drew an arrow to show I'd made the connection."*

When the students finish making connections between the text and the feature, guide them in writing a few notes that combine details from the two texts. This is a good time to return to the purpose for reading to think about what they've learned.

Prompt the students to talk in small groups: *What connections did you make between the feature and the text? How does this help you answer our essential question?*

Questions to Push Kids' Thinking

- *What did you learn when you looked at this feature? What are a few words you can write in the margins about what you learned?*

- *What are you learning as you read the text? Did you learn this from the feature, too? Or is this new information?*

- *How can you show that this detail in the text helped you understand this detail in the feature?*

- *How does this help you answer our big question?*

Finding the Right Sources

- While the pre-paired text and photograph used in this lesson can be a good starting point, moving on to texts from different sources will give your students glimpses of different ideas and viewpoints.

- Locating a text and feature that complement each other gets easier with practice. I start by identifying a text I want to work with and then searching on the internet for a complementary infographic.

- Consider additional lessons that make connection between the text and another type of feature like a map or diagram or illustration.

Lesson Idea 3

Be THIEVES to Make Informed Predictions

TYPE OF SOURCE	TIME	STRATEGY
Two texts with multiple features (e.g., title, subheadings, visuals) that can be previewed before reading	Two 40-minute lessons	Students use the THIEVES mnemonic (adapted from Manz 2002).

3

GETTING READY

1. **Select sources:** This strategy works best with texts on a similar topic that have strong features. The examples in this lesson are about the impact of the ivory trade.

2. **Study the sources:**

   • What is an important question that is answered in both texts that can serve as the purpose for reading? A question for the sample articles might be *What is being done to save the elephants?*

   • How will the title and features in the second text trigger your students' thinking about what they read in the first text?

   • Will the features or first sentence in each section of the text offer similar information, add to information from the first text in some way, or maybe even offer contrasting information?

3. **Prepare materials:** Create an anchor chart for the THIEVES mnemonic (see Figure 3.5) or copy bookmarks the students can easily reference. Provide access to both texts and a simple way for students to write notes about their predictions—on sticky notes or lined paper.

BEGINNING THE LESSON

I think of thieves as people who feel like they need something to get ahead in life. We can get ahead of an author by being THIEVES—by previewing the text before we read it. Then we will know a little bit about what we are going to learn when we read the text. When we do this again with a second text, we'll also be thinking about what we learned from the first text.

Refer to the anchor chart or the bookmark and briefly discuss each part of a text that can be previewed—title, headings, introduction, every first sentence in a section, visuals and vocabulary, and end of the text. Highlight the last step—*summarize*—by discussing how readers can summarize their predictions or what they have learned based on their preview of the text.

Figure 3.5 THIEVES Mnemonic Classroom Bookmark (Cummins 2017)

Teaching with Source 1

Let's use THIEVES to help us preview. We can start by looking at the title to think about the topic or central idea.

Think aloud with the text (see Figure 3.6). For example: *The title says, "Cracking Down on the Illegal Ivory Market Is Key to Saving Elephants." I think this is going to be about the ivory tusks that elephants are frequently killed for. A "market" is a means for selling something. Maybe the author is going to tell me about dealing with or getting rid of these ways people sell ivory illegally. I'm wondering, if it were harder to sell ivory, would people not kill elephants? I have some idea of what this text might be about and how it might help me understand our question about saving the elephants. Let's look back at the THIEVES chart to see what else we might preview.*

Continue guiding the students to use THIEVES to preview and predict. Ask the students how just previewing the text helps them begin thinking about how to answer their essential question. Capture predictions in writing, as a group or individually. Let the students read independently to confirm, expand on, or adjust their predictions and discuss or write in response to the essential question.

Figure 3.6
Examples of a title and headings that students might preview using the THIEVES mnemonic

Cracking down on the illegal ivory market is key to saving elephants

By Daniel Stiles, The Guardian, adapted by Newsela staff
11/29/2016   Word Count **852**

It appears certain that almost all legal domestic ivory markets will be closed in an effort to protect elephants.

This is plan A for a large group of animal rights and welfare organizations. The goal is to stop elephant poaching, or illegal hunting. Animal rights leaders share the belief that legal trade provides cover for illegal trade. They also believe legal sales increase demand.

Get rid of legal trade, say supporters, and fewer people will buy ivory products. Ivory is made from elephant tusks. Any elephant ivory seen for sale will be illegal. This clarity will make it easy for law enforcement to take action and for consumers to avoid buying an illegal product.

Sale Of Ivory Around The World Will End

Increasingly this is a majority position. In September, the International Union for the Conservation of Nature recommended closing the sale of ivory around the world. In October, a similar proposal was adopted at the 17th Conference of the Parties of CITES. It is the international convention that regulates wildlife trade.

Animal welfare proponents believe that selling ivory legally creates a cover for laundering. Laundering the ivory means hiding where it came from.

"It's a pity that countries with existing legal domestic ivory markets ignored the risks legal markets may bring to elephant populations," said Grace Ge Gabriel. She works for the International Fund for Animal Welfare (IFAW). The illegal laundering is made to look like legal selling, she said.

Most Countries Are On Board

President Xi Jinping of China and U.S. President Barack Obama announced last year that they would stop ivory sales, as far as national laws in each country would allow. They apparently agree with the argument of the Wildlife Conservation Society and IFAW that legal trade promotes illegal trade. Most European Union countries are also further restricting sales of ivory. In Africa, all but a few countries have banned ivory trade, as have most countries in Asia.

In the near future, there is a good chance that almost all major ivory-buying countries will have domestic ivory bans in place. So, will these bans solve the elephant poaching problem? Probably not.

Tom Milliken is an ivory expert from the wildlife trade monitoring group Traffic. He said all the protection in the world is not going to make up for poor law enforcement, widespread dishonesty and weak management.

Demand For Ivory In China Is High

I led a study of the drivers of ivory demand in eastern Asia in 2015. We found that roughly 200 metric tons (440,925 pounds) of illegal ivory were smuggled annually into China-Hong Kong from 2009 to 2014. This time is considered the peak of the elephant poaching crisis. We estimated that only about 10 metric tons (22,046 pounds) of it was processed a year to meet consumer demand. The balance of 190 metric tons (418,878 pounds) a year was most likely stockpiled by speculators. These were people apparently betting that ivory prices would remain high.

The study estimated that about 3.5 metric tons (7,716 pounds) of ivory was consumed in China legally each year. It came from ivory purchased in 2008 in Africa in a CITES-approved sale. That makes total consumer consumption about 13.5 metric tons (29,762 pounds) a year in China. Doing the math, three-quarters by weight of all ivory sold in China was illegal from 2009 to 2014.

If you count by pieces rather than weight, more than 90 percent of ivory sold in China was illegal. That's because legal outlets produce and sell much larger pieces than illegal ones. Illegal markets sell more jewelry items and trinkets, which weigh less.

Cracking Down On The Black Market

What is the plan B solution for closing the illegal market in China? The country takes in an estimated 70 percent of all poached elephant tusks from Africa. Closing the legal market will account for only 10 percent of the ivory consumed in China. The illegal ivory that consumers buy will increase from 90 to 100 percent of the market. Have the groups that want close legal ivory markets made plans for stopping the much larger black market?

I posed this question to Alexander Rhodes, head of Stop Ivory, at the 105-metric ton (231,485-pound) ivory-burning event in Kenya last April. Stop Ivory is a close partner with WCS and IFAW. He said, "Yes, that is something to think about."

Studies have found that the majority of illegal ivory is sold online in secret chat rooms and through social media sites. It is difficult to monitor those sites.

Elephants Will Still Be Illegally Killed

The goal of a total ban on legal international and domestic ivory markets is in sight. However, waving the victory flags is perhaps hasty. Elephants still have to worry that their tusks will continue supplying the huge black market. The difference is that they will come exclusively from illegal killing.

If speculation and stockpiling of tusks, rather than high demand, is driving poaching, plan B must take this fact into consideration. Plan B had better be good.

Daniel Stiles has been investigating ivory markets around the world for more than 15 years.

SOURCE 1

Teaching with Source 2

We can use what we learned in the first text to help us make informed predictions about a second text on the same topic. One way we can do this is to be THIEVES again. We'll think about what we learned in Source 1 while we preview Source 2.

Here's an example of a think-aloud with the second article: *The title is "Saving Africa's Elephants," so I'm already thinking about what I learned in the first text. I'm wondering if this article will address the legal and illegal sales of ivory.*

Continue guiding the students in previewing the text and making comparisons. Figure 3.7 shows examples of the kinds of annotations we might model writing or thinking aloud about in front of students or that students might make on their own. Ask the students to read and annotate the second text, keeping in mind the purpose for reading as well as new information they are learning.

Encourage small-group student-led discussion of the similarities and differences between the texts. You might refer back to the purpose question, asking students to think about what they learned in response to that question.

3

Figure 3.7 Excerpts from "Saving Africa's Elephants" (*Scholastic News* 2017) with examples of annotations

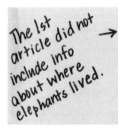

The 1st article did not include info about where elephants lived. →

The 1st article did not → mention burning ivory tusks. I wonder if this discourages the illegal sale of ivory.

JANUARY 18, 2017

Saving Africa's Elephants

→ This may have to do with ban I read about in 1st article.

China bans the trading of ivory to help protect elephants.

Last month, the worldwide effort to save elephants took a step forward when China banned the buying and selling of ivory, which comes from elephant tusks. China, the world's largest market for ivory, is the latest country to outlaw the ivory business. In July 2016, the United States toughened its laws on trading ivory.

The goal of these bans is to help save Africa's elephants before they become extinct. Global demand for ivory leads to tens of thousands of elephants being killed each year for their tusks. This latest move by China is partly the result of an agreement it made with the U.S. in 2015. That year, President Barack Obama and China's president pledged to work together to end the ivory trade in their countries.

Wildlife conservation groups have praised both countries' actions. Carter Roberts, the president of the World Wildlife Fund, stated that China's ivory ban "is a game changer for elephant conservation."

The End of Elephants?

At one time, African elephants numbered in the millions. Today, experts estimate that fewer than 500,000 are left. Years of illegal hunting by poachers have put elephants at risk of vanishing. A survey released this past August called the Great Elephant Census shows just how dire (extremely serious) the situation is. The number of Africa's savanna elephants dropped by one-third since 2007. "Sadly, wherever these animals exist in the wild, they are threatened," says Andrea Heydlauff, who works for a conservation group called 500 Elephants.

To help save elephants, nations around the world signed an agreement in 1989. That made it illegal to buy or sell most ivory taken from elephants after that year. But these rules haven't stopped poachers. Every day, about 100 elephants in Africa are

This map shows how the range of African elephants shrank from 1979 to 2012.

Jim McMahon

A Kenya Wildlife Service ranger watches over the burning of ivory tusks at the Nairobi National Park in Kenya.

CARL DE SOUZA/AFP/Getty Images

→ The 1st author said we have to crack down on illegal sales or there's no hope.

SOURCE 2

Questions to Push Kids' Thinking

- *How does what you previewed in Source 2 connect with what you learned in Source 1?*

- *Let's look at this feature* (e.g., title, heading, photograph) *in Source 2 together and think about how this compares to what we learned in Source 1.*

- *Were your predictions about the second source confirmed? Or did you need to adjust them?*

- *How do both texts help you answer the essential question?*

When Texts Are Tricky

- The topics for these two texts do not have to be exactly the same. They could simply complement each other. For example, one teacher chose an informational article on how buildings are engineered to withstand earthquakes and then a second text that was a short fictitious story about the 1906 San Francisco earthquake. Students used what they learned in the informational article to help them make predictions about what they would be reading in the story.

- Not every text has the features in the THIEVES mnemonic. Teach students to be flexible in their use of THIEVES. Students do not have to preview the source using each part of the mnemonic in a lockstep fashion, and they do not have to preview every part of the source. The goal is for students to be strategic and make informed predictions. For more information, see a blog entry I wrote on this topic at http://bit.ly/2F1kyBX.

Lesson Idea 4

Use the Coding Method to Self-Monitor and Compare

TYPE OF SOURCE	TIME	STRATEGY
Two or more sources on a similar typic	Two 40-minute lessons	Students pause to ask questions about what they just read like "Is this new information?" or "Did I already read this in another source?" or "Do I understand this?" Then they "code" their thinking while annotating the source (adapted from Hoyt 2008).

GETTING READY

1. **Select sources:** Choose two sources that are on the same topic. The examples of sources used in the lesson described below are both about the discovery of a new planet.

2. **Study the sources:**

   • What is an important question that is answered in both texts? For the two texts about Proxima b, the question might simply be *What are we learning that is current news in the field of astronomy?*

   • In the first text, what detail(s) might you model coding and thinking aloud about in front of students?

   • What notes might you jot in the margins next to the code?

   • In the second text, what detail might you model "noticing" as similar to or different from a specific detail in the first text? What notes will you jot about your connection?

3. **Prepare materials:** Create an anchor chart (see Figure 3.8) or bookmarks with the codes that students can easily reference. Provide copies of both sources for students to mark or sticky notes for students to jot

on and place in original sources. If you want more information about how to teach coding with one source, see my blog entry at http://bit.ly/2Ed550p.

BEGINNING THE LESSON

When we read more than one source on a topic, we need to ask ourselves questions like "Is this information new to me?" or "Did I already read this information in another text?" or "What do I not understand?" Jotting down codes and a few notes as we stop to ask these questions can help us keep track of our thinking.

Provide time for students to read the entire first article before they begin to reread and code their thinking.

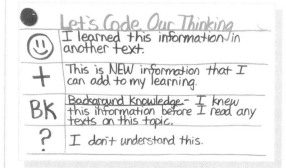

Figure 3.8 A Classroom Coding Chart (Duermit 2017)

Teaching with Source 1

Let's read the first paragraph and think about how we can code our thinking. (Read aloud or have students read independently.) *As I think about what I already know, I am thinking that this detail* (underline a detail) *is new information to me. I'm going to add an asterisk and a note to remind myself of what I learned.* (Ask students to continue reading and coding their thinking. After students have coded a few details, continue your discussion.) *Look back at your codes and notes. What have you learned? Turn and talk with a partner. Use your notes to help you.*

The text in Figure 3.9a–b shows sample codes and notes. While adding notes, think aloud. For example: *I'm going to underline "circles a star named Proxima Centauri, the same way Earth orbits the sun" because I think the new planet's location is important: the author has compared the new planet's movements around this star to Earth's movements around the sun.*

Figure 3.9a–b
Excerpt from "Another Earth?" from *Scholastic News* **(Culligan 2016), and examples of codes and notes a teacher or student might write**

4

a

News for your classroom
Daily news and current events for kids—
from *Scholastic News Online*®

News for Your Classroom > Top News > Another Earth?

OCTOBER 14, 2016

Another Earth?

Scientists discover a planet that could be home to life.

BY TRICIA CULLIGAN

For years, people have wondered whether there's life on other planets. Scientists may now be closer than ever to answering that question.

Using powerful telescopes, a team of **astronomers** (people who study planets and other objects in space) in South America discovered a new planet, called Proxima b. It orbits, or circles, a star named Proxima Centauri, the same way Earth orbits the sun. Proxima Centauri is the closest star to our solar system.

→ I know what an astronomer does. BK
→ Name of the new planet ⊕
→ It moves around a star just like Earth does. ⊕

OUT OF THIS WORLD

Scientists believe the new planet has a rocky surface and is similar in size to Earth. More important, they've determined that the distance between Proxima b and its sun gives the planet a similar temperature to Earth's. This means it could have liquid water. The presence of water on a planet makes it

SOURCE 1

Figure 3.9a–b
Excerpt from "Another Earth?" from *Scholastic News* (Culligan 2016), and examples of codes and notes a teacher or student might write

4

Then, summarize aloud what you have learned. For example: *So far I've learned that a group of scientists discovered the planet and named it Proxima b. Proxima b is like Earth in that it orbits or moves around a star. I'm wondering how else Proxima b is like Earth and if there is life on this planet.*

Wow! So if ⊕ →
Proxima b has water,
it might also have
life like Earth, too!
How do we find
out if there's water?
⑦

Another Earth?

possible for life to exist there. Scientists refer to planets like Proxima b as "Goldilocks planets" because they're not too hot or too cold, but just right to possibly support life.

Astronomers have found other Goldilocks planets in the past, but none are as close to Earth as Proxima b. Still, the new planet is 4.2 **light-years** (the distance that light travels in a year) from Earth—that's about 25 trillion miles away.

LOOKING AHEAD

Despite the long distance, astronomers hope to one day get a much better look at our newfound neighbor. But they'll need to wait until more-advanced telescopes are developed. They may also send robotic spacecraft to investigate the planet.

Paul Butler is an astronomer at the Carnegie Institution for Science in Washington, D.C. He was part of the team that discovered Proxima b. He says he can't wait to learn more about the mysterious planet.

This article first appeared in the October 10, 2016, issue of *Scholastic News* Edition 5/6.

help researchers find some answers?

> Read More

JUNE 29, 2017
O Canada!
Our northern neighbor

→ This is how we will
find out. ⊕

SOURCE 1

Teaching with Source 2

Briefly introduce the second source, shown in Figure 3.10, and provide time for students to read or look carefully at it. Then you might say, *We will understand this second source better if we think about whether the details are the same as those in the first source or whether the details are new information that we can add to our learning. We can do this by reading or looking at a part of the source and then stopping to think, "What details are important?" and "Is this new information? Or did I already learn this in the first text?" If a particular detail was already in the first source, then we can write ☺ in the margins as a code. Let's choose a part of this infographic to look at together and think about how we can code our thinking.*

Engage the students in looking at a part of the infographic and stopping to code their thinking. The infographic in Figure 3.8 shows sample codes and notes. If needed, step in and think aloud for the students about a particular detail.

After the students code their thinking and discuss their coding in small groups, remind them to "step back" from the source and think about what they have learned from both sources.

Figure 3.10
Excerpt from "Proxima B Habitability" (NASA 2017) with examples of codes and notes

4

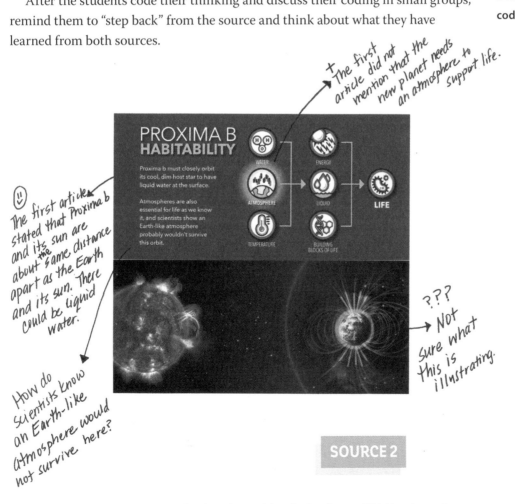

Questions to Push Kids' Thinking

- *I see you have a code for your thinking. What are a few words you can write next to the code to help you remember what you were thinking?*

- *What did you just learn in the second source? Is that the same information you read in the first source? Or is that new information? Not sure? Let's look back at the first source.*

- *I see you put a ☺ as a code. What did you notice in this source that was the same as in the first source?*

- *Let's read a chunk together and think aloud about what we've learned. Then we can think about whether that is new information or not and what code to write.*

- *What have you learned from both sources?*

When Texts Are Tricky

- Sources can be dense with details. If students are overwhelmed by the amount of information in a source, suggest that they identify and underline or mark three to five important details first and then code and write notes about just those details.

- The coding strategy can also be helpful when students are listening to audio clips or viewing videos. Encourage students to keep the same questions in mind and, when needed, to pause the audio or video clip to jot down a code and a few notes.

Lesson Idea 5

Name the Types of Details to Compare

TYPE OF SOURCE	TIME	STRATEGY
Two or more short nonnarrative texts (or excerpts) that describe something or explain how something works or occurs	Two 40-minute lessons	Students compare information presented in multiple texts on the same topic by identifying the types of details authors use to describe or explain.

5

GETTING READY

1. **Select sources:** Choose short descriptive texts tightly focused on the same topic or aspect of a topic. For example, with the two texts in Figure 3.12 (excerpts from longer books) the students were engaged in a unit of study on simple machines.

2. **Study the sources:**

   • What is a purpose for reading the two texts you have chosen? For the teacher who selected the sample texts, the purpose was simply *What types of details do the authors use to teach the reader about simple machines?* With this question, the teacher was able to teach content while also helping students compare how two authors explain a concept.

   • What types of details are in these two texts that you want students to notice?

   • If both authors use a similar type of detail, how does the information differ? How might you explain this during a think-aloud?

3. **Prepare materials:**

   • During the first few lessons, plan to work with students to generate a chart listing

types of details (see Figures 3.11–3.12). After the first few lessons, you might use the chart to make a permanent list of types of details on bookmarks that students can reference.

• Provide copies of the text that the students can mark on.

Academic Language

identify – name it

description – what it looks like

function – what it does

location – where it is

comparison – how two things are similar or different

historical connection – how it was used long ago

real-life example – where we see it in real life

Figure 3.11
Types of Details (Ballew 2015)

Figure 3.12 Examples of the Types of Details Authors Use in Science-Related Sources

Authors typically use the following types of details in nonnarrative science-related texts (Cummins 2015):

- location
- function, purpose, or behavior
- duration, or when something takes place
- physical attributes (movement or action, color, size, shape, number, texture, composition, etc.)
- construction or organization
- explanation of how something works
- real-life examples
- comparisons (including similes and metaphors)
- other types of figurative language (alliteration, onomatopoeia, and personification)
- quotes from experts (for the purpose of sharing relevant knowledge or just sharing an opinion)
- attempts by the author to connect with the reader.

For more information about introducing types of details, see a blog entry I wrote at http://bit.ly/2m2Cnsr.

BEGINNING THE LESSON

When we read more than one text on a topic, it helps to think about how authors use details to teach us about the topic. Types of details include descriptions of what something looks like or how it works or where you can find it. Two authors may use the same type of detail but in different ways. Reading both authors' texts can create a clearer, more detailed picture of what we are learning about.

Teaching with Source 1

Let's read this text once and then reread it again, stopping to think about the types of details the author is using. (Pause for students to read.)

Now I'm going to read this first sentence again and think about the type of detail the author is using. The author is telling me _____ . I'm going to underline this detail and write the type of detail in the margin. (Model underlining and annotating.) *I'll add this type of detail to our list.* (Begin list on chart paper.)

In the examples in Figure 3.13a–b, both authors describe the simple machine called a wedge.

A think-aloud for the first detail might include the following: *In this first sentence, the author tells me that a wedge is "thin at one end and wide at the other." The author is describing the physical characteristics of the wedge. I'm going to underline these words and write the name of this detail above them. Now let me think about this detail again. I learned that the wedge's size changes from one end to the next, that it is thinner on one end than the other.*

If some text does not lend itself to identifying a type of detail, think aloud about that for students. *In this sentence, I didn't notice any details that help me understand my topic better, so I'm not going to underline anything.*

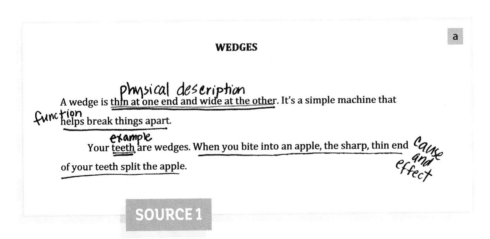

Figure 3.13a
Excerpt from
Simple Machines
(Adler 2015) with
examples of
annotations

Teaching with Source 2

We will understand this second text better if we think about the type of details the author is using to describe the topic and whether the first author used the same type of details or not. Let's read the whole excerpt of text and then go back and reread. (Provide time for students to read.)

Let's read this first sentence together and think about the type of detail the author is using to teach us about this topic. (Model underlining, naming, and annotating the detail.)

Did the first author also use this type of detail?

For the text examples on wedges, a think-aloud with the second text might include the following: *In the first text the author wrote that teeth are an example of a wedge, and in the second text the author gave the examples of the head of an ax and the tip of an arrow. This adds to my learning. Now I have several examples in my head of how everyday things are wedges.*

If students have difficulty looking at similar details in two texts, ask them to color-code similar types of details to help them visually track the information.

Figure 3.13b
Excerpt from *Machines Make It Move* (Tomecek 2003, 8) with examples of annotations

Nurturing Informed Thinking: Reading, Talking, and Writing Across Content-Area Sources

Questions to Push Kids' Thinking

- *What did you just read? What type of detail is that?*

- *How are the details in Source 1 and Source 2 similar or different?*

- *Does a detail in Source 2 add to what you learned in Source 1?*

When Texts Are Tricky

- If students identify a detail that doesn't fit into the categories you've discussed, ask them to think about what the author is trying to teach them. Name this as a new type of detail.

- Our goal is for students to use "noticing and naming" as a strategy for learning and synthesizing information, not to worry about precise labels. If students get stuck trying to label a detail, ask, *What do you think the author is trying to teach you?* or *What are you learning from this detail?*

- Not every detail needs to be named.

Lesson Idea 6

Sketch a Combination of Details to Integrate

TYPE OF SOURCE	TIME	STRATEGY
Two or more short nonnarrative (often science-related) texts or excerpts that describe something or explain how something works or occurs	One 40-minute lesson	Students combine details from two or more texts on a topic to sketch a quick illustration.

6

GETTING READY

1. **Select sources:** Choose two descriptive or explanatory texts on a narrow subject like wedges, how tornadoes form, or the layers of the Earth. These might be excerpts from a textbook, articles, or texts the students already read and annotated for types of details. These texts might build students' understanding of a topic during a unit of study in the content areas.

2. **Study the sources:**

   • What is the purpose for reading these texts? How might that be posed as a question? The text examples in Figure 3.14a–c might be read with two purposes in mind: *How do severe weather systems develop?* and *What is the impact of severe weather on humans?*

   • What is a detail from each text you can model thinking about and then sketching in front of your students?

   • How would you draw an image of the combination of details in the two texts? (These sketches should not be expertly drawn images. You want to model sketching quickly with just enough details to support learning.)

3. **Prepare materials:** Create a copy of the two texts on a single piece of paper, with additional blank space on the page for students to draw what they have learned. Once students are familiar with this strategy, you can ask them to sketch from online texts or from a source they cannot mark in.

BEGINNING THE LESSON

Sometimes it is easier to learn the information in two texts if we start by combining the details from both texts into one sketch.

Introduce the topic of the texts and briefly preview. Then provide time for students to read both texts and then regroup. You might ask them to turn and talk with a partner about what they learned from this first read and what they might include in their sketches.

Teaching with Source 1

Let's look back at the first text. What are three or four key details in the text that we want to use to sketch an image of this topic? Let's number those details and then think about how to create a sketch of what we learned.

The text examples in Figure 3.14a–c both describe how tornadoes begin and the effects of tornadoes. (Notice that my sketch is nothing spectacular—just enough to help me think and learn.) In the sketch with the texts about tornadoes, I, the illustrator, have combined details regarding the number of miles per hour winds in a tornado can travel, how far a tornado might travel, and how wide a tornado might be. Notice the similarity in details in the texts as well—both describe the tornado as funnel shaped with the narrow end touching the ground.

A teacher think-aloud for using details from the first text to begin to sketch might sound like the following: *I think there are details in this first paragraph that I'm going to try to sketch. The author writes, "A tornado springs to life when a mass of air inside a cloud is sent spinning by high winds." I think I'm going to sketch a cloud. I'll draw high winds with arrows pushing toward the cloud.*

Teaching with Source 2

Now let's look back at the second text and think about what we can add to our sketch. What are additional details or even different details that we can use? Let's number a few that we want to try to add to our sketch.

With the second text about tornadoes, a teacher might think aloud: *The details in the first paragraph are similar and I already sketched the funnel-shaped cloud, but I don't have "debris" and "dust." I'm going to add those two words to my sketch. Debris is the remains of something that has been broken down or destroyed. I'm thinking this is the remains of trees, cars, and buildings, which the first author says can be sucked up by tornadoes.* (Encourage the students to continue adding details from the second text to their sketch. After the students sketch, ask them to use what they sketched to talk about what they learned.) *Looking at your sketch, talk with each other about what you learned by reading two texts on this topic.* (Be prepared to think aloud.) *For example, I learned from both texts that a tornado is a funnel-shaped cloud or a cloud of spinning air that is wide at the top and narrow at the bottom and that touches the earth.*

[a]

A tornado springs to life when a mass of air inside a cloud is sent spinning by high winds. As the spinning column of air gathers strength and speed, it drops down as a funnel cloud. If it touches the ground, it is called a tornado. ①

Winds inside a tornado may reach speeds of more than 400 kilometers an ② hour (240 mph). A tornado may suck ③ up cars, trees, and even buildings only to smash them back down to Earth. Tornadoes usually last less than ten ④ minutes. However, they can leave behind a trail of severe destruction.

SOURCE 1

Figure 3.14a–c

Excerpts from *Weather and Climates* (Johnson 2003, 16) and "Where Is Tornado Alley?" from Wonderopolis (2017) with an example of a sketch that integrates details from both sources

[b]

Tornadoes come in all sorts of sizes and shapes. Most often, ① they take the form of a <u>funnel-shaped</u> cloud with a narrow end touching the Earth. They are usually surrounded by large clouds of debris and dust.

↳ *Wide at top, narrow at bottom*

Most tornadoes feature wind speeds under 110 miles per hour ② span about 250 feet in width and only travel a few miles before <u>dissipating</u>. The largest, most destructive tornadoes, though, can boast wind speeds of more than 300 miles per hour, span more than two miles in width and remain on the ground for ③ dozens of miles.

Scatters, disappears ←

[c]

CLOUD ① HIGH WINDS
② AIR SPINS
debris
dust
400 MPH
250 feet wide OR UP TO 2 MILES?
touches Earth = tornado
← TRAVELS
A FEW TO DOZENS OF MILES BEFORE SCATTERS OR DISAPPEARS

SOURCE 2

Questions to Push Kids' Thinking

- *What important details from the first text have you decided to include in your sketch?*

- *How can you add this detail from the second text to your sketch?*

- *How did you combine details from the two texts into your sketch?*

When Texts Are Tricky

- Sometimes there are parts of a text that cannot be sketched easily. We need to let students know that this is okay and that the point of the sketching is to deepen our understanding of the topic, not to create perfect sketches.

6

Lesson Idea 7

Use a Thematic or Main Idea Question as a Guide

TYPE OF SOURCE
Two or more sources (primary or secondary) that narrate or provide information about the experiences of individual figures or groups (including short video clips)

TIME
Two to three 40-minute lessons

STRATEGY
Students use a big question like "How was this person *innovative?*"

7

GETTING READY

1. **Select sources:** Select sources that would be helpful in answering a higher-level-thinking question you develop in advance. The text examples in this lesson were part of a middle school unit in a social studies class. The essential question the students pondered while reading these two texts as well as others was *During the Middle Ages, were the knights honorable or not? Why do you think so?* Examples of questions related to other content areas include:

   - How were members of the Jewish resistance courageous?

   - How were the civil rights activists strategic?

   - How did the actions of multiple members of the community help solve this problem?

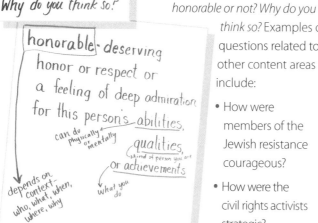

Figure 3.15 (top) An Essential Question Posted in a Classroom
Figure 3.16 (bottom) An Annotated Definition for a Key Word in the Essential Question

- What were the effects of removing the wolves from Yellowstone National Park?

2. **Study the sources:**

   - What sections of the sources might help students answer the question?

   - What is one section of the source you might think aloud about regarding details that help you answer the question?

   - In the second source, for what information might you model thinking about how it connects to the first source?

3. **Prepare materials:** Create hard copies of the texts for students to mark on and annotate. Post the essential question for all students to view. This might be on a piece of chart paper or on a whiteboard. Figure 3.15 is an example of a question that was posted when seventh-grade students were reading multiple texts about knights in the Middle Ages.

   If the question has a key vocabulary word (e.g., *honorable, courageous, perseverant, extraordinary*), post a definition for that word as well (see Figure 3.16).

BEGINNING THE LESSON

When we read more than one text on a topic, keeping an important question in mind can help us determine what is important for us to remember or think about as we read.

Teaching with Source 1

Today we are going to think about this question while we read two texts on the topic. (Refer to the posted question.) *This question can help us determine what information in a text is important for us to remember or think about as we read. Let's read this whole excerpt of this first text and then we will reread and underline details that help us answer this question. We can also jot notes about what we are thinking about the details we underline.*

After students read, demonstrate how you would think through a chunk of text, deciding what details to underline and what notes to jot. The text excerpt in Figure 3.17 includes annotations a teacher might make during a think-aloud or that students might make on their own.

Thinking aloud with this piece might sound like this: *I just learned that the Catholic Church tried to help the knights think about what it meant to be honorable by creating a list of rules called the "code of chivalry." I'm going to put a box around that phrase and I'm going to jot a note in the margin to remind me. The author also tells us the knights behaved "poorly," so I know these rules were broken. I'm thinking the Church's rules were what it wanted the knights to achieve to be considered honorable, and some of the knights did not achieve these goals.*

Figure 3.17 Excerpt from *Medieval Lives: Knight* (Butterfield 2009, 15) with examples of annotations

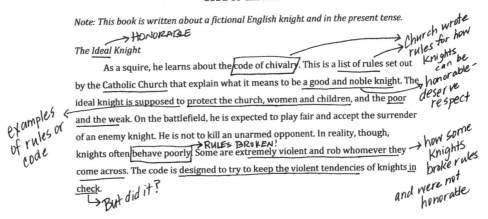

CODE OF CHIVALRY

Note: This book is written about a fictional English knight and in the present tense.

→ HONORABLE

The Ideal Knight

As a squire, he learns about the code of chivalry. This is a list of rules set out by the Catholic Church that explain what it means to be a good and noble knight. The ideal knight is supposed to protect the church, women and children, and the poor and the weak. On the battlefield, he is expected to play fair and accept the surrender of an enemy knight. He is not to kill an unarmed opponent. In reality, though, knights often behave poorly. Some are extremely violent and rob whomever they come across. The code is designed to try to keep the violent tendencies of knights in check.

→ Church wrote rules for how knights can be - honorable - deserve respect

examples of rules or code

→ RULES BROKEN!

→ how some knights broke rules and were not honorable

└→ But did it?

SOURCE 1

Teaching with Source 2

Now we are going to read a second text. As we read, let's think about details that help us answer this same question. These details may be similar to those in the first text, or they may build on what we learned in the first text.

For the example in Figure 3.18, the teacher briefly introduced the second text and then asked the students to annotate their thinking in response to the essential question. This model includes sample annotations—similar to those students might make or a teacher might step in and make during a think-aloud if needed.

Notice in this second text that the author starts with a discussion of the "vows" knights took and examples of those vows. These details are very similar to the "code of chivalry" or "rules" the students read about in the first text, so they have some background knowledge to bring to this text; they might acknowledge this in their annotations. Based on their reading of the first text, the students are probably also thinking, "The vows are honorable, but not necessarily the knights who took them."

Close by asking students to revisit the guiding question in small groups. Remind them to use their annotations and the text to help them think about what to say or support what they are saying.

Figure 3.18
Excerpt from *Le Morte d'Arthur* (Malory 2015) with examples of annotations

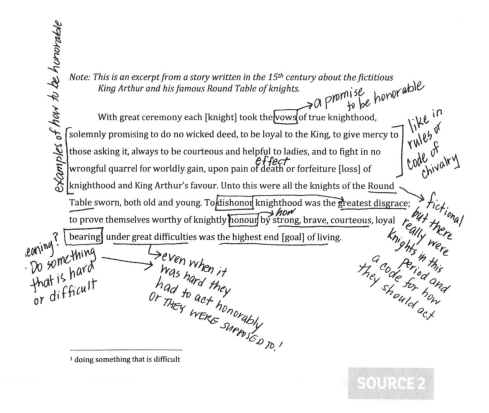

SOURCE 2

Questions to Push Kids' Thinking

- *What part of this source did you just look at closely? What did you learn? How does that help you think about our question or purpose for reading?*

- *How does what you just learned in this second source compare with what you learned in the first source?*

- *If we are thinking about the question, how does the author of this second text add to what you learned in the first text?*

When Texts Are Tricky

Sometimes there are parts of a text that do not include details relevant to the guiding question or purpose for reading. You may need to think aloud about how you decided *not* to underline particular details. In this case, a think-aloud might sound like, *When I read this section I learned some information, but I did not notice any information that was really helpful to me in answering my question, so I moved on to think about the next part of the text.*

Lesson Idea 8

Examine Texts That Have Different Purposes

8

TYPE OF SOURCE:	**TIME:**	**STRATEGY**
Two or more sources (text excerpts, video clips, infographics) on the same topic or issue but with different purposes (including primary sources)	Two 40-minute lessons	Students identify authors' differing purposes.

GETTING READY

1. **Select sources:** Identify at least two texts that have different purposes. For more information on author's purposes, see Figure 3.20. An easy way to start is to look for a current event article in which the author's purpose is to recount or tell about an event that occurred. Then find a text on the scientific or historical aspect of this topic. Both of the text examples in the lesson described below are about hurricanes and were used as part of a study on severe weather. The first one describes how a hurricane develops. The second one, though, is a first-person account of Hurricane Katrina. While both authors are writing about the same topic, they have very different purposes.

2. **Study the sources:**

   • What is an important question that both texts answer? For the two texts on hurricanes, the purpose for reading or guiding question might be *How does reading texts with different purposes help us understand a particular topic better?* Or if students are engaged in a unit focused on severe weather, the question might be *How would you describe a hurricane?*

   • How does a reader know that these texts have a particular purpose?

   • What details does the author in each text use that indicate a particular purpose? How might you explain this to students?

3. **Prepare materials:** Create an anchor chart with the different author's purposes that students can easily reference (see Figure 3.19).

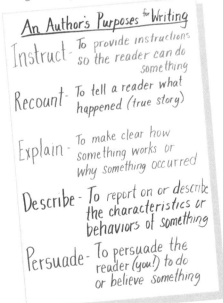

An Author's Purposes for Writing

Instruct - To provide instructions so the reader can do something

Recount - To tell a reader what happened (true story)

Explain - To make clear how something works or why something occurred

Describe - To report on or describe the characteristics or behaviors of something

Persuade - To persuade the reader (you!) to do or believe something

Figure 3.19 Classroom Anchor Chart of Author's Purposes

Figure 3.20 Clues to and Examples of Author's Purposes

Author's Purposes	Clues	Examples
To instruct	• Is the author teaching you how to do something? How do you know? • Does the author provide steps for you to follow?	• How to strap on a life jacket when a ship like the *Titanic* is sinking • Steps for making soap bubbles
To recount	• Does the author tell you a story about something that happened? • Does the author describe a series of events that took place? • Does the author include details about when something happened? Where it happened? Who was involved?	• The story of what the captain of the *Titanic* did when it started to sink • The rescue of a whale off the coast of California • Events related to the five-day march from Selma to Montgomery, Alabama, for voting rights in 1965
To explain	• Is the author teaching you about how something works? Or how something is produced? • Is the author explaining why something occurs or occurred?	• How the *Titanic* sank • How sound waves travel • The life cycle of a butterfly • The effects of the shifting of Earth's tectonic plates
To describe	• Is the author describing what someone or something looks like in a particular time and place? • Is the author describing how someone or something behaves? • Is the author describing what something is made up of?	• Description of the different spaces in the *Titanic* (e.g., decks, sleeping compartments, coal bunkers, boiler room) • Physical characteristics of butterflies and moths • Behavior of army ants • Physical properties of solids, liquids, and gases
To persuade	• Is the author trying to persuade you to do or believe something? • Is the author sharing an opinion? • Is the author making a case or arguing for something?	• People on the *Titanic* did not have to die. • Immigrants who came through Angel Island in the early twentieth century were treated unfairly. • Reducing waste and reusing items are better than recycling.

BEGINNING THE LESSON

Two authors writing about the same topic can have very different purposes or reasons for writing. Asking ourselves, "Why did the authors write these texts?" can help us think about how texts are similar or different and help us understand a topic better.

Refer to the classroom anchor chart you created and briefly discuss the types of purposes.

Provide time for the students to read the first and second texts independently or with a partner. Prompt them to begin thinking about the author's purpose while they read. Then regroup.

Teaching with Source 1

Let's look back at the first text and think about what we learned. (Pause to let students recall details from the text.) *Why do you think the author wrote this text? What in the text makes you think so?*

If students need support, project the text and think aloud. See Figure 3.21 for a sample text and think-aloud.

Figure 3.21

Excerpt from
Seymour Simon's Extreme Oceans
(Simon 2013)

During warm summer days, the sun heats the air and the water in the ocean near the equator. Warm, moist air rises and leaves a low-pressure system below, creating dense rain clouds and bringing air from the surrounding areas, where the pressure is higher, rushing into the area. Strong winds begin to spiral inward and upward. The growing tropical storm is fed and pushed by the prevailing wind.

SOURCE 1

A think-aloud might look like this:

As I read, I started to realize that the author is explaining how hurricanes form. He starts with what happens first—"the sun heats the air and the water in the ocean near the equator"— and then he talks about what happens next, as a result of the heating of the air and water—"warm, moist air rises and leaves a low-pressure system below." So he is explaining how something occurs. What do you notice that he does after that?

THINK-ALOUD

Teaching with Source 2

Let's look back at the second text and think about the author's purpose.

If students need support, lean in and think aloud again. Here's a sample second text:

> As Katrina hit land, the wind sounded like the ocean was in pain, and angry. In awe, we stepped out into our courtyard. I watched as the rain that was falling in sideways circles, ripped the roof off of our newsroom. I ran back inside, only to see a hole above my desk and rain pouring onto my computer. In a frantic rush we raced to the other, "safer," side of the building. Pieces of insulation began falling, and metal shards flew past, it felt like a combat zone with enemy fire coming from all directions.

SOURCE 2

Figure 3.22
Excerpt from a letter to the editor from *ByGeorge! GW's Faculty, Staff, and Community Newspaper* **(Groover 2005)**

8

A think-aloud on this text might sound like this: *I noticed that this was written in a first-person point of view. I think the author is telling the story of what happened to her when Hurricane Katrina hit land. She recounts what happened. What else indicates she's recounting what happened?*

After analyzing the second text, prompt students to think aloud about both texts in small groups: *How do the authors' purposes differ? How is that revealed in the types of details they include in their texts? How did both texts contribute to our learning?*

Questions to Push Kids' Thinking

- *What do you think the author's purpose for writing this text is? What in the text makes you think so?*

- *How are the authors' purposes in the texts similar or different?*

- *Could these authors have more than one purpose? Why do you think so?*

When Texts Are Tricky

- Typically, an author does not sit down to write and say, "Is my purpose to instruct, recount, explain, describe, persuade, or recount?" It is the students' understanding of the author's aim, not the terms that they use to describe it, that matters in this lesson.

- Give students opportunities to identify purposes in maps, diagrams, photographs, and videos. You might ask, *What is the creator's/developer's/artist's/photographer's purpose? What in this source makes you think so?*

Lesson Idea 9

Compare the Texts' Structures

TYPE OF SOURCE:	TIME:	STRATEGY
Two or more texts on the same topic or issue, but with different structures	Two 40-minute lessons	Students analyze texts' structures.

9

GETTING READY

1. **Select sources:** Identify two texts that have different structures. An easy way to start is to look for a text that has a clear main idea and subtopics. Then find a related text that presents a problem and solution related to that topic. Or hunt like this in the reverse order. The texts described in this lesson are both about drones. The first text is a Wonderopolis article about drones that includes a definition of drones, a history of drones, and current uses of drones. The second text is a Scholastic News article that discusses current problems with drones and possible solutions.

2. **Study the sources:**

   • What is an important question that both texts answer? For the two texts on drones, the questions in a reading / language arts classroom might be *How does identifying the different structures in two texts help us remember what we read and deepen our understanding about the topic?* If students were engaged in a unit of study regarding the roles of technology, the question might be *What is the evolving role of drones in our society?*

   • What details in the two texts reveal each text's structure?

   • Plan to use the language in Figure 3.25 if students need guidance. For example, you might think aloud for the student with a statement like "I noticed that the author introduces a problem by writing that . . ." and then cite from the text.

3. **Prepare materials:** Decide if you are going to introduce all the structures at once or just the two for the texts you selected. Create anchor charts that name some typical structures for the students to reference (see Figures 3.23 and 3.24).

> **Text Structures**
> [Topic/Sub-topic] - The author wants to teach the reader about a topic or issue. ↳drones
> After an introduction the author writes about sub-topics or different aspects of the main topic.
> → • definition of drones
> • history of drones
> • rules for safety
> • new uses of drones

> **Text Structures**
> [Problem-Solution] -
> The author identifies a problem and then explains ↳people ignore rules for using drones safely how the problem was solved or could be solved.
> → national drone registry educate users

Figure 3.23 (top)
Classroom Anchor Chart for Texts Structured as Descriptions

Figure 3.24 (bottom)
Classroom Anchor Chart for Texts Structured as Problems and Solutions

Figure 3.25 Six Common Text Structures

Text Structure	Clues	Examples

Main topic and subtopics (enumerative)	• Does the author unpack a main topic by writing about several subtopics?
	• Does the author describe or explain one characteristic of a topic and then move on to another characteristic?
		• Topic: Drones
		  ▪ Subtopics: Description of a drone, how drones are used by the military, new federal rules for drone use, future uses of drones
		• Topic: Extreme weather
		  ▪ Subtopics: Tornadoes, hurricanes, sandstorms, hailstones, blizzards

Sequence	• Does the author write about steps you need to follow to make or do something? • Does the author describe the stages of a life cycle?	• Steps for making chocolate • Life cycle of a butterfly
Chronology or narrative	• Does the author tell you about a series of events during a particular time period? • Does the author tell what happened in a story-like way?	• The Nazis' rise to power during the 1930s • A journalist's experience when Hurricane Katrina hit land
Comparison	• Does the author describe or explain how two or more things are alike or different?	• Ice caps and ice sheets • The experiences of immigrants at Ellis Island versus Angel Island
Causal relationships	• Does the author explain why something occurred? The cause and effect? • Does the author tell you about a particular event and then about what happened because of that event? • Does the author explain a chain of events in which each event occurred because of the previous event?	• Passengers on the *Titanic* died (effect) because of flooding in the bulkhead compartments, frigid temperatures in the water, and a lack of lifeboats. • When the wolves were removed from Yellowstone (cause), elk herds grew and ate the grasses that the sparrows needed for nesting. The sparrows began to disappear.
Problem-solution	• Does the author introduce a problem or multiple problems? • Does the author explain how a problem was solved or could be solved?	• Drones can cause noise pollution in quiet areas, collide with objects, and invade people's privacy; new federal guidelines are being developed to protect citizens. • Wolves were strategically reintroduced into Yellowstone National Park by a team of scientists.

BEGINNING THE LESSON

Two authors writing about the same topic can organize the information in a text very differently. Asking ourselves, "How did the author structure this text?" can help us think about what we are learning about that topic and *how two or more texts are similar or different.* (Refer to the anchor charts and briefly discuss the different structures.)

Introduce the texts. Provide time for the students to read both texts and briefly discuss the main idea and key details in each text before engaging in a conversation about each text's structure.

Teaching with Source 1

Give students a moment to review the first text, then ask, *What structure did this author use to organize this article? What in the text makes you think so?*

Be prepared to think aloud about how you determined the author's text structure. Here's a think-aloud I might use for the article in Figure 3.26a–b: *I noticed that the author's main topic is drones, but the author also talks about different*

9

a

SOURCE 1

WONDEROPOLIS
Where the Wonders of Learning Never Cease

Wonder of the Day #1531

How Can You Get a Bird's Eye View?

TECHNOLOGY — Inventions

Have You Ever Wondered...

- How can you get a bird's eye view?
- What is a drone?
- What are drones used for?

intro

As you're playing in the backyard, you suddenly hear a faint buzzing sound. Is it a swarm of bees coming your way? You listen closely and the sound gets louder. It's definitely coming from above you.

You look up and scan the skies above you. Could it be a bird? A superhero? Nope! It's a small helicopter-like device with four propellers, hovering over your backyard. What is it? A drone, of course!

People flying quadcopter drones as a hobby may seem like a new fad, but drones have been around for a long, long time. In fact, drones have been around almost as long as airplanes have been used in warfare.

definition of a drone

But what exactly is a drone? In general, any unpiloted aircraft or spacecraft could be considered a drone. Some people use another term for drone: unmanned aerial vehicle or UAV. The absence of a pilot isn't necessarily the only criterion for a drone, though.

Figure 3.26a–b
Excerpt from "How
Can You Get a
Bird's Eye View?"
(Wonderopolis 2017)
with annotations that
are clues to the text's
main topic and sub-
topic struture

9

subtopics related to the drones. In this first section, the author defines a drone, but in the next section the author discusses the first drones and how they were used by the military. What else did you notice that might support the idea that this is topic-subtopic text structure?

After the discussion, ask, *How did thinking about the text's structure help you remember what you read about this topic and understand the author's purpose?*

b

definition of a "true drone"

Remote-controlled airplanes and helicopters have been around for decades. Most people don't consider these drones, though, because a person is controlling all of their movements. To be considered a true drone, most experts believe a device must be able to perform tasks such as flying, hovering, and navigating without human input. Some level of autonomy is thus necessary to be considered a drone.

first used by military

Drones were first developed for military purposes. Drones allowed military organizations to gather information and deliver bombs without putting a pilot's life at risk in dangerous war zones. Unlike the small drones hobbyists use today, military drones can be quite large, approaching the size of regular aircraft. Drones are so useful for the military that experts estimate that a third of all aircraft operated by the United States Air Force today are drones.

describes newer drones

→ *so different*

Modern drones used by hobbyists are lightweight and run on batteries. Unlike military drones, they can only stay airborne for a few minutes before their batteries need to be recharged. Longer flying times would require larger batteries, which would weigh too much for the drone to take to the sky!

rules

More than just a fad, drones are definitely here to stay. In February 2015, the Federal Aviation Administration (FAA) began drafting rules for public use of drones for a variety of purposes. The rules are necessary to ensure the safe use of drones and to prevent accidents or interference with other aircraft.

new uses

Will drones affect your life in the future? You never know! At least one major Internet retailer, Amazon.com, wants to use drones to deliver packages to customers. Farmers are investigating ways in which drones can be used to apply pesticides or fertilizer to crops. Meteorologists have also started using drones to help monitor severe weather situations, such as large storms and hurricanes.

SOURCE 1

Teaching with Source 2

Ask students to think about the first text's structure as they review or reread the second text. Then move into a discussion. *What structure did this author use?*

The article on drones in Figure 3.27a–b includes annotations that reveal the problem-solution structure of this text. A teacher thinking aloud about the second article on drones might begin, *I noticed that toward the beginning, the author introduces a problem—"users are ignoring the rules about how to fly them safely." Actually,*

Figure 3.27a–b
Excerpt from
"Drone Control"
(*Scholastic*
News 2015) **with**
annotations that
reveal the text's
structure

9

a

for your classroom

Daily news and current events for kids—
from Scholastic News Online®

December 1, 2015

Drone Control

Do you own a drone? If so, the U.S. government wants to know about it.

This holiday season, one item is sure to show up on a lot of wish lists: drones. Up to 1 million of the small, remote-controlled aircraft could be sold during the holidays, according to one estimate. Many people across the U.S. fly drones for fun or to take photos or videos from the air. But as drones have become more popular, a growing number of users are ignoring the rules about how to fly them safely. → *problem*

SOURCE 2

In October, the Federal Aviation Administration (FAA) announced a plan to try to deal with the invasion of these small flying machines. (The FAA is the part of the U.S. government that oversees non-military aircraft.) The FAA is creating a national drone registry, or list. People will have to → *Solution* register drones when they buy them. The FAA hopes to have the registry set up by the end of this year. The registry will allow law-enforcement officials to track down the owner of a drone that flies anywhere it shouldn't.

Figure 3.27a–b
Excerpt from
"Drone Control"
(*Scholastic*
News 2015) with
annotations that
reveal the text's
structure

I noticed that the author presented more than one problem related to drones.
What other problem does the author describe? What else did you notice in the article
that indicates that this is a problem-solution text structure?

Let students talk in small groups and/or write in responses about each text's
structure and what they learned about the topic from both texts.

9

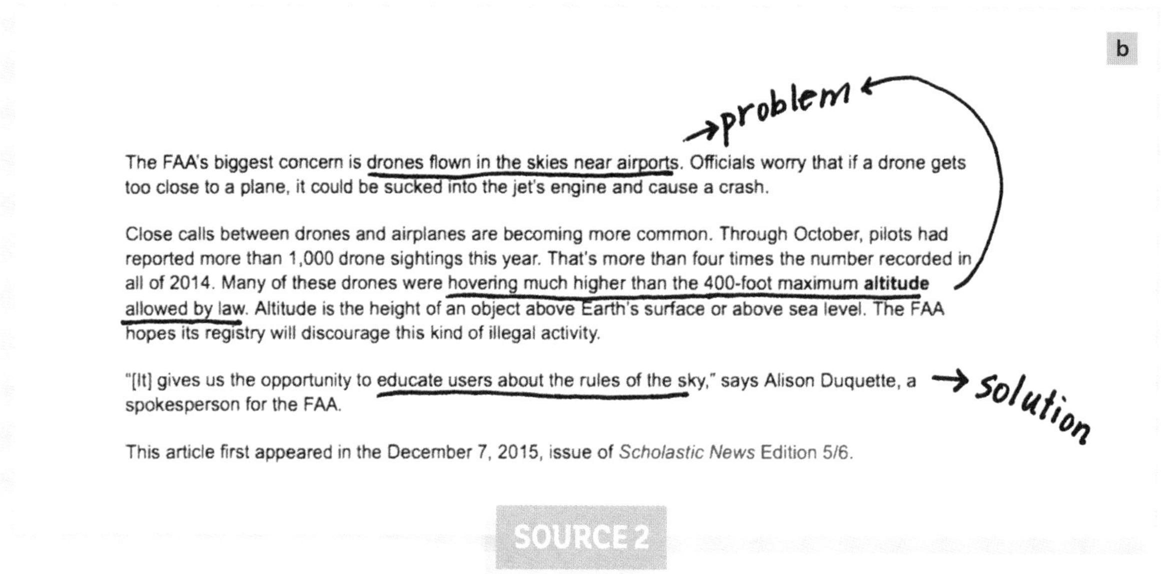

The FAA's biggest concern is drones flown in the skies near airports. Officials worry that if a drone gets too close to a plane, it could be sucked into the jet's engine and cause a crash.

→ *problem* ←

Close calls between drones and airplanes are becoming more common. Through October, pilots had reported more than 1,000 drone sightings this year. That's more than four times the number recorded in all of 2014. Many of these drones were hovering much higher than the 400-foot maximum **altitude** allowed by law. Altitude is the height of an object above Earth's surface or above sea level. The FAA hopes its registry will discourage this kind of illegal activity.

"[It] gives us the opportunity to educate users about the rules of the sky," says Alison Duquette, a spokesperson for the FAA.

→ *Solution*

This article first appeared in the December 7, 2015, issue of *Scholastic News* Edition 5/6.

SOURCE 2

Questions to Push Kids' Thinking

- *Why do you think the author wrote this text? How did the text structure support the author's purpose?*

- *How is the first text's structure different than or similar to the second text's structure? What details in the two texts make you think so?*

- *How does noticing the texts' structures help us remember what we read?*

When Texts Are Tricky

A text might have an overarching structure as well as a microstructure. If your students notice this, ask, *How do both the overarching structure and the microstructure help the author convey information?*

▍ A Few Closing Thoughts

While these lessons are neatly formatted for the purposes of this book, the actual teaching and learning that happens during these lessons can be messy. Students bring all sorts of skills and knowledge to the table when we teach. Some students may take these strategies and fly as they apply them to additional texts and in additional contexts. Other students may need more hand-holding for a while. Initially, I highly recommend choosing texts carefully for these lessons, but at some point students need to use these strategies when they identify texts on their own—which can be even messier. Chapter 5 discusses how to gradually release responsibility to students within a unit and across the year for identifying guiding questions, locating texts, and grappling with the content in those texts.

As educators, we also bring all sorts of background knowledge as well as teaching experiences to our classrooms. For some of us, teaching students to read informational sources this closely, with careful attention to specific details or aspects of texts, may be unfamiliar. Chapter 4 describes instructional moves that can support you in planning and can support your students in building pathways for learning across texts.

Supporting: *Instructional Moves That Help Students*

4

*I*n a third-grade classroom, Karen, a teacher, and Martha, a literacy coach, were exploring teaching students how to recognize the types of details authors use to describe simple machines. As part of this unit of study, they were introducing students to academic language that could be used to discuss many texts on simple machines like *function, location,* and *physical description.* Their ultimate goal was for students to create stop-motion videos explaining a particular simple machine and its modern-day use.

The initial lesson introduced the concept of simple machines and included a read-aloud of *Simple Machines: Wheels, Levers, and Pulleys* (Adler 2015). The next lesson focused on reading excerpts from multiple texts about simple machines and annotating specific types of details. Martha sent me this email after watching Karen teach:

> *She modeled the close reading and how to use academic language to identify different parts of the text. After her model she released the students to work on close reading with the objective to identify [the types of details in] two short passages. As I was observing I was*

slightly nervous [as] to how the kids would transition to independent
work, but THEY LOVED IT! The students dove right into it and were
discussing with their partners, using the anchor charts, making
illustrations, and really engaging in rich discussion around the text.

These students clearly had a sense of "I can do this!" as they "dove right into" reading, annotating, and discussing the texts. How did this happen? Karen relied on her repertoire of foundational teaching moves—tried-and-true instructional techniques that work in a variety of instructional situations. In this chapter, we'll take a close look at six powerful moves that you can use over and over again in your classroom to help your students become more independent in reading across texts.

Foundational Teaching Moves and a Gradual Release of Responsibility

During this lesson, Karen used foundational teaching moves to help students build their own pathways for learning:

- She set a clear purpose for reading multiple texts on one particular simple machine.

- She thought aloud for the students as she read a first text, providing a clear demonstration of how she processed text.

- She used language during this think-aloud that identified the types of details (i.e., academic vocabulary) the students could begin to use on their own.

- As she thought aloud, she underlined and annotated a copy of the text projected for all students to see. Her annotations named the types of details (i.e., academic vocabulary).

- With the students, she codeveloped an anchor chart that listed the types of details.

When her students moved on to continue reading and thinking with a partner, they had a clear purpose and several tools, including a lot of academic language, to use to build their understanding. Karen wasn't done after this lesson, though. Over the next several lessons, she would act as a coach or guide as students continued reading and thinking about multiple texts on the simple machines. Sometimes they would need her to step back in and think aloud again. Sometimes they would need her to be a think partner, helping the class muddle through a complex text together. Sometimes they would surprise her, teaching her something new—a strategy they developed for reading on their own or information they had learned about simple machines.

Karen's lessons were an iteration of the gradual release of responsibility. She modeled and then she began to release responsibility. This approach to teaching is not new. While there are many variations, the gradual release of responsibility usually includes some type of teacher modeling, *I do*, and then instructional steps that move the students toward independence—*we do, you do with a partner, you do alone.* But when students are reading, listening, and viewing more than one informational source on a topic, it's not just a linear progression from *I do* to *we do* to *you do.* Instead, we continually find ourselves stepping in at different points with different texts to model and guide and then stepping back to give students opportunities to work independently.

In a sense, our instructional moves should help students build pathways for learning. Imagine we want to build a pathway from one end of a small wooded area to the other. There is a diversity of plant life, including ferns, flowering herbs, grasses, shrubs, and many trees. Each type of vegetation offers new challenges to building the path. At different points during this experience, we will need particular tools—perhaps a shovel or a wheelbarrow or pruning shears or a rake. We will also need a mentor or guide, someone who has built other paths, who can coach us along the way. Our experience might include the following:

- Our mentor shows us how to use the tools and then observes and coaches us as we begin.

- If this is the first path we've ever built, we may feel clumsy using some of the tools initially, but with time, we become more efficient.

- The mentor leaves us to work on other projects but returns at different points to check on our progress.

- We come across an unfamiliar type of terrain or vegetation as we build this path—perhaps a creek that we need to build our pathway across or a mature tree with roots we do not want to disturb. Our mentor acts as a think partner as we brainstorm how to proceed or steps in to show us how to start. Then our mentor steps back again to give us a try at continuing on our own.

- Throughout this whole process, we keep an eye on our purpose—to build a pathway from one end of the wooded area to the other.

- Along the way, though, we can't help but learn a tremendous amount—not just about building paths but also about the diversity of life in the woodland.

It's the same experience for our students as they begin to tackle reading and understanding multiple texts on the same topic. There's a clear purpose for building the pathway. As the mentor or more knowledgeable other, we introduce tools the students will need to build pathways of learning across texts. We may show students how to build parts of the pathway, and we may act as think partners and build some of the pathway *with* our students. If there's a rough spot or unfamiliar terrain along the way, we may step back in to show the students another tool or strategy and then step back to give them a try. As we build, we always keep an eye on our purpose.

Shared Practice, Guided Practice, and Independent Practice

This process and the ensuing relationship is more complex than *I do / we do / you do.* Informational texts are tricky, complex, and, on top of that, frequently about topics that we, the teachers, have not mastered. Now add reading, listening, and viewing multiple sources to the equation. The teacher and the students have to forge the path together. In a sense, both the teacher and the students are members of a community of practice—a community of strategic readers, note takers, discussants, and writers, working with complex sets of sources and tasks on a regular basis.

Within this community of practice, there's time for *shared practice*, in which the teacher may model or think aloud for the students or may engage the students in thinking aloud together. This shared practice is an opportunity for the teacher and students to be think partners. I'm always surprised at what students reveal to me when I invite them to think *with me* about a text or multiple texts. They frequently reveal insights I had not thought of in my own reading of the texts. Other times their thinking reveals a need for me to help them clarify or think more deeply about a text.

Shared Practice (Teacher and Students Build Together)
- The teacher states the purpose(s) for reading, viewing, and listening to more than one source on a topic and briefly introduces the sources.

(As described in Chapter 5, shared practice may include a collaboration between the teacher and students to develop purposes for reading.)

 * With the students as think partners, the teacher and students explore how to use a particular strategy or activity to think about multiple sources or take notes about those texts or write in response to those texts.

 * In this exploration, the teacher may do a "think-aloud" using *I* statements to reveal how the teacher is making sense of a source, and/or the teacher and students may engage in a "shared think-aloud" in which both the teacher and students share their thinking.

Within this community of practice, there's also time for *guided practice*, in which the teacher leans in to observe, assess, and confer with individual students or small groups at the point of need.

Guided Practice (Students Build with Teacher as Mentor)

 * With the teacher fully present to provide support, students work on their own or with a partner or small group.

 * The teacher actively leans in to observe, assess, and coach at the point of need.

 * When coaching, the teacher may engage in another think-aloud or in a shared think-aloud together with the student.

Finally, a community of practice includes time for *independent practice*, in which the students go it alone.

Independent Practice (Students Build Alone)

 * This practice happens any time the student is reading, taking notes, writing, or conversing with peers *without* the teacher present to coach.

 * This practice may happen before or after a coaching conference with the teacher.

 * This practice may happen when students transfer the skills they have developed with one set of sources and tasks to a new set of sources and tasks.

A series of lessons may start with shared practice and then move on to guided and independent practice. When there's a tricky part, though, the teacher and students may need to regroup and engage in shared practice again. For example, in a fifth-grade classroom studying ecosystems, after the teacher engaged the students in a shared discussion of a diagram, the students easily moved to independent practice analyzing a second diagram in small groups. When the students had to tackle a text excerpt from a book, though, the teacher realized they needed to regroup and engage in a shared think-aloud, closely reading and annotating the first few sentences in the text with the teacher as a think partner before they could move forward on their own.

Moves That Support Students at Every Stage

A critical part of this community of practice is the tools that are used *throughout* a lesson or series of lessons—the purpose, the texts, and the language or academic vocabulary used to make sense of the texts. (Notice that these tools are cognitive as well as physical.) My colleagues and I have found that we have to consistently tap each of these during shared and guided practice to deepen students' understanding of multiple sources during independent practice. For example, it's not enough to post and state the purpose at the beginning of the first lesson with the first source. We have to consistently refer back to this purpose during the shared and guided practice.

On the pages that follow, we'll unpack six essential instructional moves that will help you support your students in shared and guided practice. We'll use the purpose, the source, and academic language as constants in a community of practice focused on tackling multiple complex informational texts on the same topic. This chapter also provides some guidance regarding assessing students formatively as they work independently:

Instructional Move 1: Sustain a clear purpose for reading multiple sources on the same topic.

Instructional Move 2: Give a prominent role to the actual sources and the notes taken.

Instructional Move 3: Use language that has generative value while thinking aloud *for* and *with* your students.

Instructional Move 4: Use visual scaffolds to support vocabulary development.

Instructional Move 5: During guided practice, confer with individual students to assess and teach at the point of need.

Instructional Move 6: Support students as they write in response to multiple sources.

Sustain a Clear Purpose for Reading Multiple Sources on the Same Topic

A clear purpose for reading can make the difference between productive and unproductive reading and thinking for many students. The purpose acts as a guide for determining what details or information is important to think about in multiple texts. Even when I've established a purpose for reading with students, I've found that I have to refer to the purpose for reading over and over again, during the shared and guided practice, to help students develop the mindset of "I'm reading for a clear purpose." Below are some suggestions for how to do this.

Shared Practice

At the beginning of the first lesson, post the purpose(s) so that all students can view it throughout the lesson.

As shown in Figure 4.1, write the purpose for reading, viewing, and listening to multiple sources on a piece of chart paper or the whiteboard for all students to view. Sometimes I ask the students to write the purpose across the hard copy of their source. These purposes are designed to be relevant across texts and can also be part of a unit of study. Notice that I included quick, kid-friendly definitions to help students clarify the purpose. At the beginning of a lesson, you can simply start by introducing a question like "What are the advantages and disadvantages of burnt forests?" and then stating, "We are going to be reading multiples texts that help us think about and answer this question."

During a teacher think-aloud, model looking back at the purpose as you decide what's important to consider in the source(s). Continue doing this as you engage students in a shared think-aloud.

As you think aloud about what is important in a text, make it clear to students that you intentionally look back at the purpose and consider it as you start to think carefully about a first or second or additional source. These are examples of what this might sound like at different points in the shared practice part of a lesson:

Figure 4.1 An Annotated Purpose for Reading

- *Before I start reading this second text, I want to remind myself why I am reading this text as well as other texts—what's my purpose? To help me, I can look over here at the chart with the purpose written on it.*

- *I just read a difficult chunk of this text with a lot of information. I think I need to go back to my purpose for reading to help me determine what is important, what I really need to pay attention to in this text.*

- *Let's review the purpose for reading together before we determine what is important in this next section of text.*

Guided Practice

Review the purpose for reading, viewing, or listening before students begin to read and take notes independently. If needed, ask them to write the purpose at the top of their copy of the sources or on their notes and then talk with a partner about how they will use the purpose to determine what's important.

In one classroom, students were studying how the act of "investigation" is part of the daily practice of scientists. As a class they engaged in a shared reading of one text excerpt that revealed how a scientist engaged in investigating a topic. Then on their own, the students were tasked with looking for additional excerpts, in self-selected texts on a particular scientist or project, that revealed how that scientist engaged in investigation. Before pursuing this task, small groups met to discuss their purpose for reading. The teacher prompted them with the following question:

> *While you are reading, what will you be looking for? In other words, what is your purpose for reading? It's not enough to just say, "I'm looking for a place that says that the scientist is investigating something." Instead, consider, "What does investigation mean? What might investigation look like in your text?"*

Their conversations might sound like the following:

> **Student 1:** *So we need to keep reading in our books and we need to find a chunk of text that does this.*

> **Student 2:** *Right. We need to find a place or a page or something that shows how the scientist investigates.*

Student 3: *And* investigate *means (looks up at posted definition) "to examine, study, or inquire systematically in an attempt to learn the facts about something."*

Student 1: *Okay. So in my text, the scientist is trying to figure out why the golden frog is disappearing. I think she's going to do something to "investigate" this, like she's going to come up with some plan and take steps to figure this mystery out.*

During coaching conferences, prompt students to look back at the posted purpose. Be prepared to think aloud about how you had to look back at the purpose to think about what was important.

A class of students was reading multiple biographical sketches and other essays about strong women who lived on the western frontier of the United States in the late nineteenth century. Their purpose for reading was to "compare and contrast how the different women were extraordinary." When the teacher leaned in to confer with one group, she noticed the students were caught up in comparing when two of the women were born. The teacher recognized that this comparison did not help the students think more deeply about how the women were extraordinary. To redirect the students, she asked them to refer back to the purpose that was written on the whiteboard: "How were these women extraordinary?" The students quickly realized that they were off track and moved forward in their discussion.

Independent Practice

Below are some general guidelines for what you should observe when students are working independently, sustaining a clear focus on their purpose for reading:

- Students' comments during small-group discussions reveal a focus on the purpose for reading.
- Students' notes are mostly relevant to the purpose for reading or include details that help the students make sense of the text as they grapple with the purpose for reading.
- Students' writing reveals thinking related to the purpose for reading.

If you're not seeing this kind of independence when students are working on their own, step back in and use the earlier strategies to reinforce this skill with students.

Give a Prominent Role to the Actual Sources and the Notes Taken

Continually referring back to the sources and to the students' notes reinforces their learning, helps them clarify their thinking, and also helps them develop the language they need to discuss and write fluently about what they have learned. This seems obvious, but frequently during conversations or when writing responses, students try to recall what they have learned *without* referring to the sources or their notes. There is a place for recalling information from memory, but early on as students grapple with and begin to master content, the sources and their notes can be helpful. I remember watching a group of eighth-grade students who had just read and annotated a science text on how cells divide get up from their desks to talk in small groups about what they'd learned and most of the students *left their notes behind*. I quickly moved them from independent practice back into shared practice by regrouping and asking a student to come to the front and model having a conversation in which we continually referenced our notes to think about what to contribute next.

Shared Practice

If appropriate, provide copies of the sources to make it easy for students to read across sources.

If possible, place the texts side by side so that students can easily look at both. One teacher, Nicole, started creating "storyboards" with the texts, copying multiple texts, including excerpts and diagrams, onto one large sheet of paper during a unit of study focused on how weathering and erosion shaped the landscape of California (see Figure 4.2). For video clips, she

Figure 4.2 A Student Using a Storyboard to Work with Multiple Sources

included a blank box on the storyboard for students to take notes.

Project the source for all students to view. As you model or engage students in thinking together with you, write on the text(s) that is projected.

Students need visual and auditory scaffolds for how to interact with the texts. Texts can be projected with document cameras, using Smart Board software, or through interactive televisions. As you and the students think aloud about parts of the text, mark on the text in front of them (see Figure 4.3). This annotated text becomes documentation of thinking and learning that you can refer back to later during conferences or during follow-up lessons.

Engage the students in a discussion about how to look at sources online or in a book and think about what to write in their notes.

At some point, students need to learn how to read a source like a section of an article or a table with statistics without a hard copy of that source to mark on. One of my colleagues who had provided hard copies of sources for a while tackled this transition by having an explicit discussion about this with her students. She started by asking,

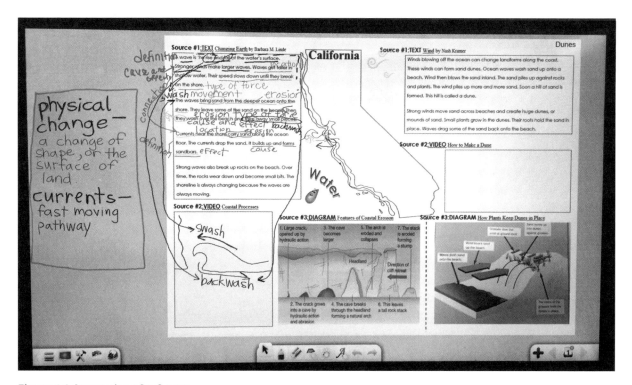

Figure 4.3 Annotations On-Screen

"What do we need to do differently if we do not have a copy of the text to mark on?" She was pleasantly surprised by the effortless conversation that ensued. The students gave suggestions based on the strategies they had been taught, like creating an inquiry chart (as described in Chapter 5) with the guiding questions written across the top and the sources listed down the left-hand side. The teacher also noticed that students used similar strategies when they took the state assessment online, using scratch paper to take notes about the different sources.

Guided Practice

During conferences, coach students in looking back at the source to clarify or to provide evidence to support their thinking.

The following was a conference a teacher had with a student who was comparing extraordinary women who lived on the western frontier of the United States in the late nineteenth century. He had read a biographical sketch about Mary Fields and another about Calamity Jane:

> **Teacher:** *So what have you noticed about these two women?*
>
> **Student:** *Both women disguised themselves as men.*
>
> **Teacher:** *How does that show that these women were extraordinary?*
>
> **Student:** *Well, Calamity Jane dressed as a man so she could get jobs that women usually could not get like working on the transcontinental railroad. Mary Fields . . .* (The student pauses, unsure of what to say.)
>
> **Teacher:** *What can you do to help yourself?* (The student sits, stumped.) *Why don't you look back at the essay about Mary Fields to help you make your point? Let's look together.*

The student looks back and realizes the author of the article did not state that Mary Fields *disguised* herself as a man. The author just stated that she dressed *like* a man. Looking back helped the student revise his thinking and think more critically about why both women dressed as men. If the student does not look back at the source successfully, you may need to move into a shared think-aloud.

Coach the students in how to use their annotated texts or notes to engage in conversations.

With a class of students reading multiple texts on ecosystems and using an inquiry chart to keep notes, I asked a student to volunteer to be my partner in conversation about what we had learned. I placed my notes on the document camera for all the students to view and the student brought her notes to the front of the room. I let the student start the conversation about what she'd learned in response to the three questions we had written on the inquiry chart. Then I demonstrated how I'd listened to my student-partner and how I referenced my notes to think about what I could add to the conversation. My think-aloud for the students and my conversation with the student sounded something like the following:

> **Student:** *I learned that plants are producers of energy and animals are consumers of energy.*
>
> **Teacher:** (Speaking to the whole group.) *I'm looking at my notes and I see that my partner probably pulled that information from the first text we look at, the diagram. What can I add? (*I pause to look at my notes.) *I think I'm going to use information from the first and second diagram to add to our conversation. (*I point to the place in the notes to which I am referring.) *I notice that she told me about two groups of organisms involved in the function of an ecosystem, but I also have notes on a third organism, so I think that would be good to add to our conversation. (*Then I begin speaking to my partner.) *In addition to consumers and producers, there is a third group of organisms in this process—the decomposers. The first diagram didn't tell us much about the decomposers, but the second diagram gave us more information. Decomposers like bacteria break down dead plants and animals to make food for the plants. That makes me think they are just as important to the ecosystem as plants and animals.*

Over the course of four or five exchanges, I continue by prompting the student-partner to think about what we had both said and to reference her notes before contributing to the conversation. During this experience, the student-partner and I had the opportunity to demonstrate not only how to think across texts but also how to express our ideas clearly and how to build on each other's ideas as well. For many students, this is a missing piece in their "turn and talk" conversations. Many times, students simply share what they are thinking. They may even repeat the same information. They don't always *listen and contribute.*

Independent Practice

Below are some general guidelines for what you should observe when students are actively using the notes they have taken:

- Students' comments during small-group discussions include references to their notes and to the texts.
- Students' comments during discussions include thoughtful analysis of what their peers are saying and questions about their peers' notes and annotations.
- Students' writing references the texts read in a meaningful way.

If you're not observing these behaviors, plan for additional shared or guided practice to support the students.

Use Language That Has Generative Value While Thinking Aloud *for* and *with* Your Students

In this context for learning, language that has "generative value" is any language that can be used over and over again to think about multiple sources on a particular topic. What if a teacher said the following during a think-aloud about a second text introducing the concept of an ecosystem?

> *When I started looking at this diagram, I remembered what I did to look carefully at the first diagram about ecosystems. My eyes moved to the top left-hand corner. I noticed right away that this illustrator also included a sun with an arrow leading down to a type of plant— just like in the first diagram. I remember that in the first diagram, the plant was labeled as a producer of energy. So I'm thinking that both diagrams are going to give me information about the role of the sun or solar energy and plants, which are producers of energy. Next I noticed that . . .*

The language in this think-aloud is very intentional. The teacher has used vocabulary like *diagram, top left-hand corne*r, *illustrator*, and *arrow* that can be used to look at many other diagrams. She has also used language that reveals thinking strategically— *started looking, my eyes moved, I noticed, next I noticed*—language that reveals steps students can adapt for themselves. And she has integrated domain-specific vocabulary—*ecosystems, sun, solar energy, plant, producer*—vocabulary that students need to learn and use over and over again as they read additional texts on a particular topic like ecosystems.

A teacher think-aloud with language that has generative value happens when the teacher reveals how she makes sense of a source. In the case of reading, viewing, and listening to multiple sources on a topic, during a think-aloud the teacher needs to refer to previous sources she analyzed as she thinks aloud about a second or third or additional source. This typically includes making *I* statements like those used in the think-aloud above. A "shared think-aloud" occurs when the students and teacher engage in a similar way. The teacher may start with an "I noticed" statement and, if appropriate, say, "This made me think of the other source we read because . . ." Then the teacher prompts the students to share their thinking by asking, "What did you notice?" and "How does that connect with previous sources we have read?" The teacher helps the students extend or clarify their thinking with questions like "What in the sources made you think that?"

It is tempting to start a lesson by asking students questions about the sources like "What was similar in these two excerpts of text?" or "How was one author's purpose different from the other's?" These questions serve to *assess* understanding, but they do not teach students *how* to do this. Some students may be able to jump into the conversation when you ask these types of questions, but many may need you to model for them first with language they can adopt and begin to use on their own.

Figure 4.4 shows some transferrable language you can model when discussing diagrams, table, maps, and video with students.

Figure 4.4 Examples of Language We Can Use to Help Students Unpack Sources

Generative Language for Different Source Types

Diagrams
Encourage students to look at the diagram systematically, moving in one direction: down or up, left or right.

- *When I see a diagram, I start by asking myself, "What is the author of this diagram trying to teach me about?"*
- *I know that diagrams are usually organized from top to bottom and left to right, so I'm going to try to figure out where I should start and then I'm going to work my way to the bottom or to the right.*

Tables
Encourage students to determine the author's purpose and then to make systematic sense of the table.

- *When I see a table, I remember that the author has a purpose for this. I'm going to start by thinking about this chart's purpose. Let's read the title of the chart and see what else we notice.*
- *Usually, tables are organized from left to right. I'm going to start at the top left-hand corner to help me make sense of this chart.*

(continues)

Maps

Maps are developed to reveal a particular idea or concept. Encourage students to think about the main topic of the map before they begin to glean specific information from the map.

- *I'm sure you all noticed already that this is a map. Not all maps are alike, though, right? A map has a big idea or focus. I'm going to read the title of this map and look at the other details to see if I can identify the main topic of this map.*

- *Now that I have thought about the focus of this map or what it is mostly about, I'm going to look for and think about specific details in the map and how they tell me more about the map's topic.*

Videos

There can be a lot of information shared in just a few seconds of video. The creator of the video's content might include text features like maps, diagrams, and so forth. Encourage students to "hear" information and "view" information. Strongly encourage them to replay small portions of video as needed over and over again until they understand the information well enough to take notes.

- *Now that I've watched this whole video or a big chunk of it, I'm going to listen to the first part of this video and stop the video when I hear or see a piece of information that might help me answer a guiding question.*

- *I just heard a piece of information that I know will help me answer a guiding question, but I don't remember what it was exactly. So I'm going to listen to just those few seconds again.*

- *I just saw a chart pop up on the video. I'm going to go back and pause the video at that point so I can look at the chart more closely.*

Useful Analogies

During instruction with multiple sources, analogies for what happens for us as learners when we think across multiple sources can make the learning process more concrete for students. In Chapter 3, I introduced the THIEVES mnemonic, an activity used to help students think strategically about how to get ahead of the author to make informed predictions. Below are other examples of analogies my colleagues and I have used with students that can be referred to again and again as students read multiple texts on the same topic. This language potentially has value beyond one learning experience.

Determining What's Important: Making Pasta

When we cook pasta, we put the pasta in boiling water, and after it has softened, we put the pasta in a colander in order to drain the water. We do this because we want to eat the pasta and not the water. It's the same way when we are reading to determine what is important. Depending on our purpose for reading, there are pasta details and water details. The pasta details are the details that help us understand the purpose for reading.

For more information on introducing this analogy to your students, see my blog entry at http://bit.ly/2CvXJEW.

Growing from Using Multiple Sources: Tree with Foliage and Extensive Roots

My colleague Nicole developed an analogy about healthy trees: they grow from seedlings to mature plants with extensive foliage and deep roots (see Figure 4.5). Similarly, as we read each additional text or source on a topic, we develop deeper roots of understanding and more foliage. The texts act as sunlight and nutrients for our growth. The roots and foliage are what we learn as a result. If we don't read multiple resources, we may be weak and not strong enough to continue growing and thriving.

Figure 4.5 Nicole's Student Using the Tree Analogy to Capture Her Learning

Richness of Thinking: Layers of a Cake

You can have a single-layer cake or you can have a multi-layer cake. What would you rather have? As we read each additional source on a topic, we are adding a layer to our understanding—which means we have an even richer cake to share with others.

Text Structure: A Building's Purpose

A building has a particular purpose. For example, the purpose of a house is usually to be a home or place for a family to eat and sleep. The purpose of a grocery story is to be a place where food and other items can be purchased. A building's structure is based on the purpose of that building. If you visit a home, you would expect to see rooms for sleeping and a room for cooking. If you visit a grocery store, you would expect to see separate sections for different types of food like vegetables or meat that you might buy. Similarly, an author's purpose drives how she structures a text. If she wants to instruct someone on how to make a birdhouse, the author may use a sequence text structure, listing the steps in numerical order. If an author wants to persuade someone that global warming is an issue, she may use a problem-solution text structure or a cause-effect text structure. For more information on introducing this analogy to your students, see my blog entry at http://bit.ly/2Axxnk9.

Shared Practice

Using language during a teacher think-aloud that reveals how you made sense of a second or additional source.

In one classroom, a group of students was studying whether naturally caused forest fires should be allowed to burn or not. Their purpose for consulting multiple sources was to learn the pros and cons and then develop their own argument for or against letting forests burn.

The first source they grappled with was a video created by the USDA Forest Service that describes how the black-backed woodpecker thrives in burnt forests on wood-boring beetle larvae. The students watched this short video multiple times and took notes on a two-column chart with the headings "Pros" and "Cons." The second source was an excerpt from *Fire Birds: Valuing Natural Wildfires and Burned Forests* (Collard 2015). After the students read the excerpt, the teacher stepped in to think aloud about the similarities and differences between the video and the text excerpt. In the following think-aloud, notice how the teacher makes very explicit what he noticed about the two sources:

> *In this second source, I noticed that the first paragraph is mostly about the wood-boring beetle. In the video, though, the narrator did not give us much information about the beetle—in my notes I just have that the black-backed woodpecker eats the beetle larvae. In this second source, though, I learned about how the beetles are drawn to the burnt forest in the first place. So this second source provides me with some new information that I can add to what I learned from the first source.*

Model with language that reveals how you decided what to write in your notes about the source and how you connected those notes to previous sources.

In the lesson on whether natural forest fires should be allowed to burn or not, the teacher continued his think-aloud by sharing what he decided to write in his notes:

> *I think I'm going to use a few details from the first paragraph to make a note about the pros of burnt forests for the wood-boring beetle.* (He pauses to look back at the text.) *I'm going to write, "Wood-boring beetles lay their eggs in dead trees" and "When the eggs hatch, the beetle larvae eat the dead wood." In my notes from the video, I'd written that the dead trees are a home for the black-backed woodpecker. Now I'm going to draw an arrow from my note*

about the beetles and their larvae to my note about the tree's being

a home for the woodpecker because the dead trees are a home for

the beetles and larvae, too.

At some point, draw the students into thinking aloud with you. Be prepared to ask more than one question to help students clarify and extend their thinking and to provide sentence stems to help students articulate their thinking.

Prompts that are helpful when we want students to think aloud with us include the following:

- *Keeping in mind what we learned in the other sources, what did you notice?*
- *What in this source makes you think that?*
- *What conclusions can you draw based on what you noticed?*
- *How does this help us answer our purpose for reading?*

Consider providing sentence stems to help some students get started. Examples of sentence stems used during the lesson on forest fires might include

- The first and second source both included details about . . .
- In the first source I learned that . . .
- But in the next source I noticed that . . .

Guided Practice

During a conference, coach students in stating not only what they learned but how they are making sense of multiple texts. Provide sentence stems as needed.

The prompts and, if needed, the sentence stems listed in the shared practice would be helpful in a conference with a small group or individual as well. In the classroom studying naturally caused wildfires, the students read a third source, an article from Newsela by the U.S. National Park Service (2016) on the role of wildfires in an ecosystem. In the transcript below, notice how the teacher prompts the students to expand on their thinking:

> **Teacher:** *So tell me about what you have learned from this article*
>
> *regarding the pros and cons of letting wildfires burn.*

Student 1: *Actually, the article starts by telling us how the wildfires get started.* (The student looks back at the text.) *The author says that fire gets started by* (cites from the text) *"the combination of heat, oxygen, fuel, and an ignition source."*

Teacher: *So how is that the same or different from the first two sources?*

Student 1: *Well, the video and the excerpt from that book kind of skipped the basics—how fires get started. The authors just went into the pros mostly. This author kind of wanted to let us know how it all gets started.*

Student 2: *And the author also tells you that a lot of fires* (looks back at the text and cites) *"90 percent" get started by humans.*

Teacher: *Oh, so now you have specific information about the difference between naturally caused wildfires and man-made wildfires. How might that help you make an argument for or against wildfires?*

Student 2: *I think when we write our argument, we have to make clear that we are talking about naturally caused fires and how those kinds of fires happen. We have to do that before we even talk about the pros or cons.*

If the student is clearly struggling to make connections across sources, shift from asking the student questions to revealing how you do this. Then draw the student into thinking aloud with you.

If you attempt to prompt a student who is at a frustration level, step in and think aloud. You may not have "planned" this think-aloud. That's all right. It's good for students to see you muddle through a text. For example, in the classroom studying the pros and cons of wildfires, there might be a student who is struggling with making connections between the first two sources and the third source on wildfires. The student might benefit from hearing the teacher think aloud about how he made connections between the sources. He might say:

There's a lot of information in this article. I'm going to take a minute and just reread the first section. Will you do that with me? (**Pauses while he rereads.**) *I'm just going to think about what I learned in this section and compare that to what I learned in the first two sources. I might have to look at your notes for the first two sources to help me. Let's do this together. In the first section, I learned about . . .*

The students might also benefit from gentle coaching on how to say what they are thinking. You might provide sentence stems that fit what the students need to say, as suggested earlier.

The focus here has been on the teacher's use of language that students can make use of on their own. We want students to take on the kind of thinking across texts that we have modeled for them or prompted them to do. This kind of thinking will aid them during independent practice.

Independent Practice

Some general guidelines for what you might notice students doing independently are below. During small-group discussions or as part of written reflections on their learning, students make comments about the content they have learned from multiple texts and *also* about how their thinking emerged as they read additional texts. You might hear students make comments like the following:

- *When I watched this video, I realized that I had not heard that information in the first source.*

- *When I read this source, I realized that it answered a question I had when I watched the video.*

- *Both of these sources helped me answer my first guiding question but provided nothing to help me with this other question. When I looked at this diagram, though, I found some information to help me, information that wasn't in the other two sources.*

- *All the sources gave me the same information, so I think I have enough information now. For example, in the first source . . .*

If you're not noticing these types of comments, move back into shared practice and intentionally highlight moments when you notice yourself or a student using this kind of language.

Use Visual Scaffolds to Support Vocabulary Development

When students are learning from multiple sources on a topic, it is helpful to teach the academic vocabulary as well as the domain-specific vocabulary. For example, during a unit of study on weathering and erosion, when students are thinking across multiple sources, they need to be able to recognize when an author has described a *cause and effect* of erosion or when an author is *explaining* how weathering occurs. Terms like *cause and effect* and *explaining* are academic vocabulary students can use in multiple contexts across the school day.

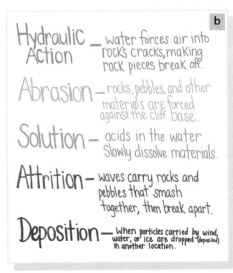

During this same unit, students also need to recognize that when the author describes how sediment or other substances settle at the bottom of the riverbed, that is an effect of erosion called *deposition.* So in addition to understanding and using general academic vocabulary that can be used in multiple school settings, students also need to grasp domain-specific vocabulary like *deposition, erosion,* and *weathering* that can be used for that particular unit of study.

Understanding both types of vocabulary helps the students recognize and explain what they are learning: when students explain *deposition,* being able to use the words *cause and effect* makes the task easier. Another benefit is that both types of vocabulary can be used to help students examine multiple texts during this unit of study.

As a result, when you plan a unit of study or a series of lessons with multiple sources on the same topic, it is helpful to generate a list of academic and domain-specific vocabulary the students may need to understand and access as they read texts. Post these words with student-friendly definitions in a place where all students can easily and continually reference them—this might be in large print on a piece of chart paper or on a bookmark. Figure 4.6a–b shows anchor charts a teacher created for students to use during a unit of study on weathering and erosion. The words and definitions were added to the list

Figure 4.6a–b Classroom Charts Supporting Academic and Domain-Specific Vocabulary

as students developed a need for them. Refer to Figure 3.9 in Chapter 3 for a good example of academic vocabulary.

During shared practice, reference these scaffolds to support your reading and thinking; during guided practice, prompt students to do the same.

Shared Practice

Develop and introduce anchor charts or bookmarks with academic language students can reference during the teacher think-aloud or the shared think-aloud.

At the beginning of the unit of study on *weathering* and *erosion*, the students might be introduced to these two terms in the first source they read or view. The teacher might think aloud about starting an anchor chart in the following way:

> *Let's start a list of vocabulary words we can use to describe what we are learning. Our guiding question has the vocabulary words* weathering *and* erosion, *and we just read what these words mean. I think we might need to recognize when authors are describing weathering and erosion in the sources we consult. Those are two words we can write in our annotations or in the margins of sources to help us remember what the author is teaching us. I'm going to start a chart with these two words. Will you help me think about how to define these words using the source we just read?*

A little later, the teacher might step in to think aloud again by saying the following:

> *I noticed that sometimes the author defines a word. An example of this is when the text says, "A wave is the rise and fall of the water's surface." I think we should write "definition" on our list of words we can use to help us think about texts.*

Guided Practice

During conferences with students, prompt them to reference the visual scaffolds.

Examples of prompts that might be helpful include

- *Take a moment to look at our anchor chart. Are there any words on our anchor chart that might help you explain what you just read?*

- *How did you use the vocabulary on the chart to help you think about this part of the diagram?*

- *I noticed you jotted in the margins a word from the anchor chart. Why did you decide to do that?*

If a student is struggling, be prepared to think aloud about how you read the source and referenced the chart:

> *There is a lot of information in this diagram. I am going to try to look at part of it and use the words on our list to help me think about what the author is teaching me. Let's do this together.*

Independent Practice

Below are some guidelines for what you might notice as students begin to use the vocabulary with the support of the list and beyond:

- When students work in small groups, they actively reference the chart or bookmark or other scaffold you have created with them.

- Students ask you if you can add another word to the list and are able to explain why they think an addition is necessary.

- Students are using the vocabulary appropriately in their annotations and discussions.

Look for this type of independence to develop over time. Continuous engagement with scaffolds like anchor charts during shared and guided practice should grow students' independence in using these tools as well as in acquiring the vocabulary.

During Guided Practice, Confer with Individual Students to Assess and Teach at the Point of Need

During guided practice, leaning in to listen to individual students talk about their learning or to visit with them about what they have written is an opportunity to launch students forward in making sense of multiple sources, their notes, and their writing. When you are engaged in the messiness of teaching students to read, view, and listen to multiple sources on the same topic, keep in mind the steps for conferring—*assess*, *affirm*, and *extend*—to help you lead a more efficient conference.

Assess

Start conferences by checking in with students on their current thinking. Generally, I will say to a child, "Tell me about what you are learning right now." Another option is to tailor my first question to what we did during shared practice. For example, if I just gave a mini-lesson on recognizing when I have read similar details in a previous text, I might start a conference with "What have you noticed in this text that is similar to other texts we have read?" Then I listen to determine where the student is in his understanding. I tend to ask myself three questions:

- What does the student say that reveals understanding of this particular source?

- What does the student say that reveals his thinking about this text as well as other sources?

- What does the student say that reveals how he has thought about a source or sources strategically?

Based on what I learn when I lean in to listen, I determine what I need to do next. If you lean in to confer when a student is engaged in writing in response to multiple texts, these three questions can be used to think about the student's written response as well.

Affirm

Next, we affirm students when they have successfully made sense of a source orally or in writing, and we want to help them clearly articulate what they did. We give them language they can use to explain how they made sense of more than one text on a topic. What we say may depend on what we focused on during the shared practice part of the lesson. Chapters 3 and 5 include examples of prompts or language we can use during conferences. The chart in Figure 4.7 includes a few additional examples of affirmations in conferences.

If you learn this from the student . . .	Then your affirmation might sound like this . . .
The student seems to understand the source.	*It sounds like you have made sense of this source. You paraphrased or put into your own words what you are learning from more than one source.*
The student seems to be synthesizing information from more than one source.	*It looks like the notes you have jotted helped you think about more than one source. I see the arrows you have drawn to connect details from the two texts. What you just told me about your learning seems to combine details you learned from these sources.*
The student is struggling to integrate ideas from more than one source in the conversation with you.	*So you have read both sources and it sounds like you have thought about each one because you just shared details from both. Let's think together about how these details can be combined.*
The student reveals a strategy used to make sense of more than one source.	*It sounds like you are making sense of this second source by thinking about what you learned from the first source. Your coding and the notes you wrote in the margin show me that you are making connections between sources.*

Figure 4.7 Affirmations in Conferences with Students

Extend

After affirming the student (even if she is struggling), decide on a teaching point that will move her forward in her learning. You may just encourage the student to continue doing whatever she was doing already to understand one or more sources or to write about her understanding of those sources. For struggling readers and writers, you may need to step in and think aloud in that moment. Your think-aloud can serve as a model for making sense of one source, for thinking about multiple sources, or for thinking about conveying an idea in writing. Then invite the student to continue thinking aloud with you. After you have done this, articulate for the student what you did together and what she needs to do to carry on. It might sound like this:

We just made sense of the text together. I needed to reread and unpack that super-long sentence. I thought about the many details in that sentence and compared those details to what I already knew from previous texts. You and I both noticed a detail that we had read in a previous text, and then you marked it with a code and wrote a note. That helps you remember what you learned in this text when you go on to the next text.

Sometimes a pattern of need will surface as we meet with several individual students. You might notice that several students are struggling with the same section of a text or with the use of a particular strategy. At this point, I suggest regrouping with the class to help them all *extend*. For example, I was in a fifth-grade class studying ecosystems. They were reading their fourth source on the topic, and during several conferences the students revealed being "stuck" in their understanding of a particular paragraph. The author had stated that species of plants and animals in a shortgrass prairie have adaptations that help them survive in that particular ecosystem. The two students I met with did not understand that the author was providing "examples" to illustrate this point—the prairie grasses have long roots that can soak up water deep underground and the prairie dogs burrow underground to stay cool. I realized this might be a problem for several students and regrouped for a quick mini-lesson. This included projecting the text for all students to view, thinking aloud about what the author was doing—providing examples to support an idea—and modeling jotting notes about this in the margins of the text. During this think-aloud, I also referenced a previous source, a diagram focused on a different ecosystem, and discussed how that source provided examples as well. The students quickly began recognizing "examples" of ideas as they continued reading and consulting other sources. After this quick mini-lesson or shared practice, though, I moved back into guided practice—pushing the students to work independently and starting to confer with individuals again.

Support Students as They Write in Response to Multiple Sources

Students may have previous experiences writing in response to individual informational texts. The less familiar task may be writing in response to *multiple* sources. When students write to respond to multiple sources, they have to do everything they'd do in a response to a single source—focus on the given purpose; determine a structure; draft and revise. However, they also need to determine the importance of ideas and synthesize concepts from multiple sources, navigate multiple authors' points of view, *and* check their responses against multiple texts. Our students need varying levels of support depending on their familiarity with the genre they are writing in and their mastery of the content. We can support students by writing part of a response together and then conferring with students as they continue writing on their own.

Figure 4.8 is from a shared writing I did with a small group of fourth-grade students after they read and took notes on two sources. As described in Chapter 2, the small group of students read two short articles with their teacher about municipal public officials—one that described the duties of these officials and another that described public officials' responses to the water crisis in Flint, Michigan. The students took notes from both texts about what public officials do to support their municipalities. The writing task I gave the students was to choose someone they know and write a letter to that person convincing him or her to run as a public official. The task required students to use what they had learned from both sources to convince this person that he or she would be an effective public official. We wrote a rough draft of a letter together. Then this shared writing experience served as a mentor experience for students as they wrote an additional letter to a person of their choice on their own.

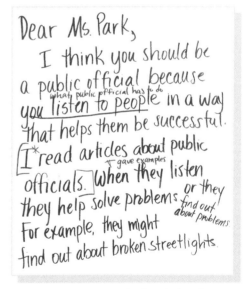

Figure 4.8 A Letter Drafted with the Class

Shared Practice

Write together with the students, acting as the scribe and the coach.

When I met with the small group to think about writing a letter, we started by thinking about who we would write the letter to and then quickly reviewed the basic parts of a letter like the greeting, body, and closing. Next I coached the students to think aloud about how they might start the letter by saying, "What do we need to tell this person first? Let's think about our topic." As we moved through writing the letter together, I continued to prompt them with comments like "Well, now that we have introduced what we want to talk about, what can we share with this person that we learned from our sources? Let's look back at our notes and think aloud about what we might write."

If needed, help students formulate sentences that make sense by providing examples of language they might use.

Some of our students, while they can communicate easily with us on the playground or during other conversations throughout the day, struggle to write in the language of informational or nonnarrative texts. When students struggle to formulate sentences, provide them with language they might use. For example, if a student is struggling to state what he learned from the two sources about public officials, you might give him stems to start like "In both of the articles I read, I learned that . . ." or "The first article included facts about . . ." or "What I learned in these articles made me think about . . ." The student repeats the stem and then fills in the rest. You might also give the students the language they need to finish an idea like "on the other hand" or "but in the second article." The trick is to provide just enough support to help them formulate a sentence or idea.

Unpack what you did as a group during the shared writing.

In the image of the shared writing in Figure 4.8, you'll notice notations like "gave examples." These notes were written after the shared writing experience, when the students and I discussed what we had done as writers to communicate our ideas. This practice is helpful when you confer with students who are "stuck" in their writing. Determine what would be helpful to your students to notice, and make notes about this on the shared writing. You might make notations as simple as "introduction," "body," and "concluding statement."

Guided Practice

Assess, Affirm, Extend

As you do when you lean in to confer with students about their reading, determine one point you can affirm them on and one teaching point you can engage them in to move them forward. When I consider teaching points, I ask myself the following questions:

- *Do they need support in making their writing make sense?* You might need to ask them to refer back to their notes and talk about their learning in an effort to understand the content of the sources better before writing.

- *Do they need to work on making their writing fluent?* If they are struggling with syntax or how to use nonnarrative language correctly, they might need to orally rehearse a sentence before writing.

- *Do they need you to push at the edge of their writing ability?* If they are writing easily, they might need you to suggest a way to make their writing more sophisticated, like explaining an example from the source and so forth.

Start a conference by asking students to read aloud what they have written so far or a portion of what they have written.

When students read aloud what they have written so far, they frequently notice mistakes on their own. You might see them pause or fill in a missing word as they read. When students self-correct or notice an error, affirm this and then help them as needed. You might say, "I noticed that you paused right there. What are you thinking you might need to do to revise your writing?"

Help students formulate sentences aloud before they write.

As noted in the shared practice suggestions, some students may need support in articulating sentences that are fluent and that make sense. If you notice this during a conference, here are some prompts you might use to launch students forward:

- *Let's look at your notes and think about what you might say.*

- *So when you looked at your notes, you noticed what you need to include in this sentence. Let's think about how to say that.*

- *Could you start by saying . . . ?*

- *What else can you add to that?*

Independent Practice

Below are some general guidelines for what you should observe when students are tackling writing across sources:

- Students' writing reveals an awareness of their audience and their purpose for writing. This might include a clear topic sentence.

- Students' writing integrates details from multiple sources.
- If appropriate, students make clear that they are writing about information from multiple sources.

If you observe that students, tasked with writing independently, are tending to rely on details from one source or are struggling to make their thinking clear, provide additional learning experiences in which they can engage with you in shared and guided practice.

A Few Closing Thoughts

Synthesizing information from multiple sources and then sharing what we have learned is a complex task that requires many skills to accomplish. There is so much we can do to sustain students as they take on thinking carefully about what they are learning from multiple sources. As teachers, we have to be willing to act as facilitators, mentors, partners, and coaches, stepping in and back as needed. Opportunities for shared and guided practice can help students as they build pathways to learning.

Releasing Responsibility:
Student-Led Research with Inquiry Charts and Other Scaffolds

5

In the earth science middle school classroom I'm visiting today, each student has self-selected a major land formation—the Grand Canyon, for example—and is researching how weathering, erosion, and deposition influenced its formation. Eventually they will develop a model that reveals their learning, but at this point they are spending the bulk of each period engaged in independent research, using inquiry charts or I-charts (Hoffman 1992) to keep track of their questions, sources, and notes. To launch each day's period, the teacher, Micheline, begins by asking a few students to share an "Aha!" moment that occurred the previous day during their research. Today, when called on by his teacher, Andrew shares the following:

> *I noticed that I was having trouble researching my question and I wanted to change my topic, and then you helped me unpack the question. It was too big. I needed to break it down into smaller questions. "Unpacking" is what helped guide me to better questions, and I found a lot of helpful information to answer those questions that I put on the I-chart. It was really the unpacking that allowed me to persevere and find what I needed to find.*

After Andrew shares, another student speaks up and shares a similar anecdote. Then Micheline turns to the class and summarizes what she thinks is important for their peers to notice:

Did anyone else find that unpacking or stopping for a moment and saying, "Let me unpack my topic, let me generate more questions, let me take a broader perspective" is what they needed to do yesterday? That's always a great suggestion. If you feel stuck, generating more questions about your topic or about what it is that you want to overcome in your research is going to lead you onto the right path.

Andrew's thoughtful comments on his own learning might sound unusually mature for a middle school student. This is no accident. His teacher has been actively helping the students take control of their own learning. This is the ultimate goal for our instruction, but it is a hard goal to reach. Think about what is involved when students tackle making sense of multiple sources in pursuit of constructing and applying knowledge.

On their own, students need to be able to

- generate a topic
- generate questions that are just right in scope and that are also researchable
- locate a variety of sources
- vet those sources for relevance and truthfulness
- paraphrase information from sources and then take notes
- synthesize information within and across sources
- transform all of that information into knowledge.

Along the way, the students also have to be able to

- continually make plans for how they will find information
- unpack questions that are too big
- abandon questions because they are too small or not researchable
- skim, scan, and read or reject resources
- struggle productively to make sense of complex texts (instead of abandoning)

- realize when they have gathered enough information to answer a question
- figure out what to do when new questions arise.

And they have to do all of this while staying focused on the point of their research, which may include one or more of the following:

- meeting a purpose for learning (i.e., standard, learning target, goal)
- learning about a topic they are interested in
- preparing to present or communicate what they learned (e.g., producing a podcast, developing a website, writing a paper, presenting at a conference).

In Chapter 4, I used the analogy of building a pathway as a way to think about how we support students in reading and understanding more than one text on a topic. At some point, however, we have to let students take more control of pathway building if they are going to become independently engaged in learning for themselves. To begin, they may build only part of a pathway you started together. Or they may take fuller control—deciding where a new path will begin and end, planning steps for building the path, determining which materials will be used, and then beginning.

This doesn't mean they can't use a mentor or consultant along the way. Wouldn't it be helpful if they visited the spot where we are building a path of our own and watched for a few minutes? What if they checked in with us to see what new materials or tools we have tried lately? Or what if they asked us to stop by to problem solve for a few minutes? And then once we're there, what if they asked us to stay for a bit to give it a go together before we head out?

As we help students become independent learners, we want them to understand that "independent" doesn't have to mean "completely alone." In the real world, we rarely tackle entire projects on our own—even if we have a lot of experience with what we are doing. We lean on others at different points for advice and wisdom. We might find a website or text online to consult, or we might watch a video on YouTube. Or we might touch base with a friend or colleague who might be able to help. What happens when we do this—when we interact with texts or people to problem solve or think about our project—even in the smallest way? We are able to return to our project and move forward productively. More importantly, though, the experience of gleaning information from others and then applying what we learned to our own project *expands* our knowledge of the world.

How Do We Nurture Student-Led Use of Multiple Sources?

We begin with the end in mind. What do we want our students to be able to do as a result of this research? Write a script for and produce a podcast? Write an argument to submit to the editor of a local paper? Write a letter to a policymaker? Develop a model that demonstrates a science-related concept? With this end in mind, think about information the students will need to learn in order to take on this project or task. For example, if students are going to develop and use a model that reveals the effects of weathering and erosion on the Grand Canyon, they will need information about how this landscape has changed over time. However, they may also need to develop some initial background knowledge. What is weathering? What is erosion? What is the difference between the two? Questions like these can drive the students' research.

We introduce students to tools that will help them track their learning and organize their notes. There are lots of ways to do this, but my colleagues and I have had the most success by introducing inquiry charts or I-charts (Hoffman 1992). As a result, this is the primary tool I refer to in this chapter. Typically, the I-chart has the questions or purposes for research listed across the top and the sources the student has located listed down the left-hand side (see Figure 5.1). As students read or view each source, they can take notes that answer particular questions in the corresponding box. In some cases, the last row is used to summarize the student's learning.

Figure 5.2 is an example of an inquiry chart that might be completed by an elementary student, and Figure 5.3 is an example of an inquiry chart that might be completed by a middle school student. In both charts, you'll notice

- The guiding questions head the columns and the sources head the rows. Thus, there is a reminder for students to look for answers to each guiding question in each source.

- Some sources have more information for a particular guiding question than others do.

- The first source line is reserved for students' prior knowledge ("What I already know"), giving them an opportunity to name what they know at the beginning of the process and to see new learning at the end of the process.

Figure 5.1 Minimized Inquiry Chart

	Question #1	Question #2	Questions #3
What I already know about the topic			
Source #1			
Source #2			
Source #3			
Summary			

- The notes in the table are just enough to help students recall what they've read—words and phrases rather than sentences and paragraphs. Keeping notes short will help students synthesize information from multiple texts.

- The final row, "Summary," is for synthesizing what students have learned about each guiding question, drawing from all the information noted in the chart. These responses are in the students' own words, not quotations from the sources.

You'll also notice some additional complexities in the middle school model:

- The topic is more controversial.

- The final column is reserved for possibilities for additional lines of inquiry ("Questions I might want to do more research to answer").

Figure 5.2 Possible Elementary I-Chart

African Elephants	What are interesting physical features of the African elephant?	What does the elephant eat?
What I already know	• Big animals • Long trunks	• Grass and trees
Grandma Elephant's in Charge, *Martin Jenkins, 2003*	• Biggest land animal • Male can weigh more than 6 tons or as much as 10 adults	• Juicy melons • Salt • Mostly eat grass, leaves, twigs
Video: "Baby Elephants," San Diego Zoo Kids, 2011, http://kids.sandiegozoo.org/videos/baby-elephants	• Calf--weighs 200-250 pounds or one adult man! • Trunk--4,000 muscles and two fingers at the end • Females smaller than males	• Bark of bushes and trees • Babies drink milk from mother
"African Elephant," National Geographic Kids, 2014, http://kids.nationalgeographic.com/animals/african-elephant/#african-elephant-mud-family-baby.jpg	• Trunk--7 feet long! • Two fingers at end of trunk used to pick up things like berries • Can use their trunk to make loud noise to warn others	• 300 pounds of food every day!!! • Leaves, grasses
Summary	I learned that elephants are the biggest animal on land. The males can weigh as much as ten adult humans, but the females are smaller. The calves weigh only about as much as one adult man. Their trunks are seven feet long and have two fingers at the end that can be used to pick up things like berries. They can also use their trunks to make a really loud sound and warn other elephants if danger is nearby.	Elephants eat a lot of food. They eat more than 300 pounds every day. They like grasses and parts of trees like bark, twigs, and leaves. Sometimes they eat melons and salt. A baby or calf just drinks milk from its mother.

How do the members of the elephant family interact?	What problems do elephants face?
• Mothers take care of babies? I'm not sure	• I don't know
• Calves play with each other • Mother elephants in Africa take care of their babies and other elephant's babies • Father elephants do not stay with the mothers and babies • Grandmother elephants in Africa remember a lot□where the water holes are and where juicy melons are • Grandmothers tell the other elephants what to do	• They are hunted • People are farming where the elephant used to live • Only half a million left
• Boy calves trunk wrestle • Girl calves run and chase each other • Adults let babies climb on them • Adults watch babies while they nap	• Hunted for their tusks
• Hug each other by wrapping their trunks together • Use their trunks to help another elephant out of the mud	• Hunted for their tusks
The father elephants do not stay with the herd of mother and baby elephants. The mothers take care of their babies and other babies. They watch over the babies when they nap to make sure they are safe. The calves are playful. They climb on the adults. The male calves play a game called "trunk wrestle." One calf wraps his trunk with the other calf's trunk and then they push back and forth. The female calves run and chase each other. The elephants hug each other by wrapping their trunks together. The grandmother elephants are in charge of the herd of mothers and babies. They show the other elephants where the water holes and juicy lemons are.	Elephants are being hunted and killed for their tusks. People sell their tusks, which are ivory. People are also farming where the elephants used to live so there is not enough room for the elephants.

Figure 5.3 Possible Middle School I-Chart

Topic: African Ivory Trade	What is the problem?	What is being done to solve the problem?
What I already know	• A lot of elephants are being killed for their tusks because they are made out of ivory	• Countries try to catch the poachers
Video: "Last Look: James Baker on Saving the Elephants," CNN, January 2017, www.msn.com/en-us/video/tunedin/last-look-james-baker-on-saving-the-elephants/vp-BBy5r4q	• 35,000 African elephants killed every year for their tusks • 20% African elephants killed in last ten years • Tusks made of ivory, which can sell for up to $1,000 per pound	• China not letting people sell ivory legally anymore • James Baker, former secretary of state, has been trying to get global ban on ivory sales since 1989
"Saving Africa's Elephants," Scholastic News, January 2017, http://magazines.scholastic.com/news/2017/01/Saving-Africa-s-Elephants	• Some experts say only 500,000 African elephants are left, but there used to be millions • Number of African elephants has dropped by one-third since 2007 • 70% of illegal ivory ends up in China • Some ivory sells for $1,500 a pound • U.S. is the second-biggest market for ivory	• In 1989 there was a ban by countries all over the world, but it didn't stop poachers • 2016 new U.S. law says that most ivory sold must be at least 100 years old□so supposed to stop new ivory being sold • Some countries like Kenya are burning illegal ivory that has been confiscated□to discourage poachers
"Cracking Down on the Illegal Ivory Market Is Key to Saving Elephants," Newsela, November 2016, https://newsela.com/articles/save-elephants-plan/id/24303/	• Bans do not work because of ineffective law enforcement, dishonest people, and poor management • 90% of ivory sold in China between 2009 and 2014 was illegal	• Some organizations (like International Union for the Conservation of Nature) think that if we get rid of the legal market, then when we see ivory, we will know it must be illegal • 2016□China and U.S. committed to stopping the sale of legal ivory • Most countries in Europe, Asia, and Africa have banned legal sale
Summary	There used to be millions of elephants in Africa, but now some experts say there are only half a million left. Just in the last ten years, the numbers of elephants have dropped by 20-33%. The elephants are being killed for their ivory tusks, and that ivory can be sold for $1,000 to $1,500 a pound. (That sounds like a lot!) Countries have banned the legal sale of ivory, but this does not always work because of ineffective enforcement of the ban or dishonest people.	In 1989, a lot of countries banned the legal sale of ivory, but this did not stop the poachers. Now most countries have banned or still have bans on the legal sale of ivory. Last year the U.S. started a new ban on ivory. You can only sell ivory in the U.S. if it is at least 100 years old. Some groups like the International Union for the Conservation of Nature think that if countries ban the legal market, then when people sell any ivory, we will know that it must be illegal. Some countries are burning the illegal ivory they take from the thieves, hoping this will discourage poachers.

What are the viewpoints presented?	Questions I might want to do more research to answer
• I don't know--a lot of people say we shouldn't kill the elephants	
• James Baker believes the U.S. has to lead the ban or other countries won't ban • Baker believes these animals are "majestic creatures" that shouldn't be sold • CNN.com must agree a global ban is good—they did not share a different side of the story	• What is ivory used to make besides little statues?
• There's a subheading in the article called "Hope for the Future"—author is feeling hopeful • 2015—32 tons of illegal ivory seized	• How do they keep track of number of elephants?
• Ban on legal sales will not help if countries do not have a strong plan to stop the illegal sale of ivory • Author estimates 200 tons of illegal ivory was smuggled into China and Hong Kong from 2009 to 2014—that's about 50 tons a year • Author did a study on illegal ivory	• What does "poor management" of the bans mean? • Do we know how many elephants have been killed since 2014?
The authors of these sources seem to believe that elephants should not be killed for their tusks. Many people like the former secretary of state James Baker believe the ban on legal sales will be helpful. The author of the last article believes that if countries don't have a stronger plan to crack down on the illegal market, though, there will be no hope for the elephants.	

Students can use this chart flexibly, making adjustments as needed. For example, in the middle school classroom I described earlier, the students decided to add an extra column on the far right side to jot new questions or ideas that surfaced as they analyzed each source. Some students decided to fold the column on the far right over to the left so they could add more information to the back of the chart. Some students decided they should sketch information from a particular source instead of writing bulleted notes. In the student charts in Figure 5.4, the notes are color-coded. In a fourth-grade classroom I visited, the students decided they wanted the questions listed down the left-hand side and the sources across the top so they could see details from multiple sources side by side. Each of these anecdotes reveals students using the charts as *tools* for learning.

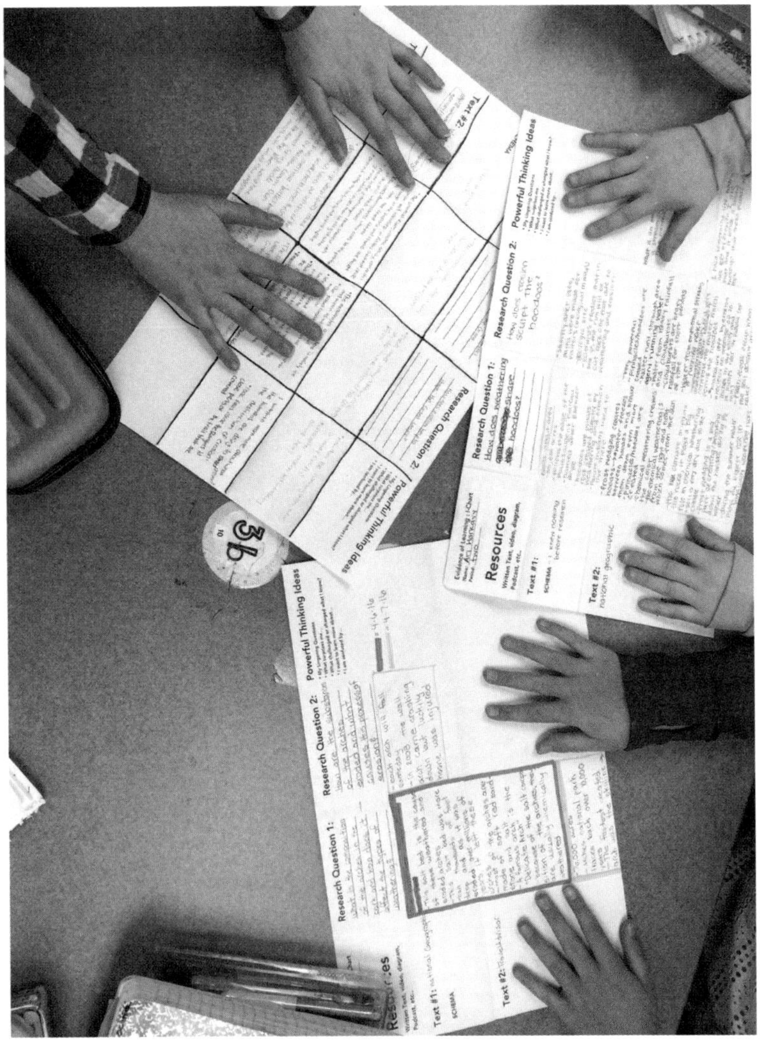

These charts are easy for students to use as they take notes *and* as they begin to think about their final project, product, or task. In a fifth-grade classroom where the students were tasked with creating an EdPuzzle for their peers on a particular Native American tribe, the students started by using a colored pencil to circle the details on the I-chart that belonged together (see Figure 5.5). As they drafted scripts for their audio files, this helped them think about which details overlapped and which details needed to be combined.

Finally, we nurture the growth of independence by providing instruction that supports learners. At first we might offer a lot of support, but gradually we have to release more responsibility to

Figure 5.4 Middle School Students Work with Their I-Chart

Nurturing Informed Thinking: Reading, Talking, and Writing Across Content-Area Sources

Sarah

@ Apache "Sorce"	① Where was this tribes primary homeland? What was the landscape or environment like?	② How did the environment influence what they ate? And their housing?	③ What did they believe? How was their religion or spirit life influenced by their location? (Ceremonies)	④ How were their arts and crafts influenced by their location?
Epic-picture pages	• Apache lived through Arizona, Colorado, New Mexico, and Texas, and Mexico • territory about the size of California • lived in a desert area • not much water around	• house called a Wickiup • entrance was low • made out of grasses • ceiling was tall enough for them to stand • made of trees	• one ceremony honors childs first pair of moccasins • child walked to the east in new clothes and shoes • this makes sure he has a good life	• sewed shells, glass, and turquise beads into clothing and shoes • also made beaded jewelry • made woven baskets • made arts and crafts • they had important uses
Epic-text pages	• territory in southwestern U.S. • has many mountains, deserts, canyons, and rivers near by • they were rich in minerals • lived in many bands all called the Apache	• Very roomy inside • didn't usally have furniture • easy to make and take down • moved quickly and leave little to show where they had been • made a "U" shape	• they let their hair grow long because it was bad luck to cut it. • they believe plants, animals, and humans had powers • prayed (sang, and danced) • Medicine men led people in special events • Apache honored one's life childhood old age	
They Call Them Apaches (Article) W.M. Akers	• Apache moved from one place in the summer to one place in the winter. • Used horses	• moved from one place to gather foods then they would move somewhere else to hunt. • Different kinds of houses • Wikiups, teepee, and hogan • teepees: triangular • Wikiups: 8 foot tall wooden frames with brush • Wikiups and hogans used for winter • would keep them warm • They used blankets (moccasins, etc.)	• Proud of Past • Take on modern lives • Still remains exciting	• Doesn't talk about Arts and Crafts.
The Apache Indians text pages by Bill Lund		• They gathered honey too • Teepees are covered in animal skins. • Used bows and arrows to hunt	• Still remember traditions • Mountain Spirit dance, are important to them • wore spotting masks for ceremonies • spit clothes on fire • only wore bottom shirt made of	• known for their baskets • use them to gather food and water • made them from parts of plants • called a tus • weaved so tightly their baskets can hold water • have a glossy finish
The Apache Indians picture pages by Bill Lund	• lived in a grassy environment • many trees around • grass is green	• might have eaten wheat like grasses • usually green • house have long entrance • very tall ceiling	• have many spirits • spirits are good or bad • anything in nature has a spirit • religon is part of daily life • ceremonies are a official • preformed by a di-yin • di-yin is a religious leader • Apache people sometimes participate in ceremonies	
Native Americans Festivals and Ceremonies Apache page 35-36		• Had owls as a resource	• had ceremonies for the comming of age for them in corn meal and clay • Had ceremonies for White Woman she is the first woman • she survived the great flood in a shell, her two spit cover the tribe from enemy, Owl Man Gaint • she met her younger self when she was old she merged into her younger self • Boys ceremonies include drinking dancing around trees, learn songs have vision • Feast after all ceremonies • Ears noses get pierced	
Apach Indians 1145 Video			• before and after hunting they preformed feasting and religos rituals • would not eat bear because they thought it was considered evil • say prayers over bone of animal • use sand masks for religous ceremonies • they had a spiritual rain dance	• used seed bead for decoration in clothing • they were vibrant • put them in diagnal lines

Figure 5.5 I-Charts Become Tools That Belong to the Students

the students for their learning. For example, when students first engage in research, we may provide questions to guide their analysis of sources. Later, we may generate questions with them. Further on, they may generate their own questions. Releasing responsibility does not mean we abandon students at the end, though. As long as they are in our classrooms, we can find teachable moments that can help them grow even more. This means that whatever point we are at in releasing responsibility, we still continually observe our students, noticing what they need and then instructing them accordingly. For example, let's say you notice several students are generating questions but the questions are too big, like "What was the culture of the Comanche tribe like?" You might provide a mini-lesson that reveals how to "unpack" questions like this one. You might model looking up the definition of a word like *culture* and thinking through what that really means in order to formulate smaller questions like "How was art a part of the life of the Comanche?" and "How were the Comanche's spiritual beliefs influenced by where they lived?"

Instruction that supports the development of independence is the focus of the rest of this chapter. There are three areas of instruction in which we can help students along the way:

1. identifying the purpose for learning and generating topics and questions for research

2. locating and vetting texts for relevance and truthfulness

3. grappling with complex texts in multiple modes and taking helpful notes.

For each area, I provide a continuum for gradually releasing responsibility to students as well as suggestions for how to help along the way based on your observations. At some points, these suggestions drill down to working with a single text, but all of them are included here to support student-led research, our ultimate goal when engaging students with multiple texts on a topic.

Identifying Topics and Questions

Chapter 2 discussed the critical role a purpose for reading stated as a guiding question can have in helping students determine what is important in multiple sources. Up front we may generate those questions, but at some point students need to generate the questions for themselves. The continuum in Figure 5.6 is an example of how we can gradually release responsibility to students for generating their own questions and, even before that, identifying the topic of their research.

There could easily be more points on this continuum. For example, the teacher might identify one or two of the questions for research and then each student might generate a third. Later on the continuum, the teacher and students might brainstorm topics together and then each student chooses one. Students might also work with partners or small groups along the way as an additional scaffold. It is up to you to decide the degrees of structure and independence you'll provide for your students. It

Within a unit of study and/or across the school year

| Teacher identifies topic and questions. | Teacher identifies topic. Teacher and students brainstorm list of questions and students choose from list. | Teacher identifies larger topic and students identify subtopic to research. Students generate their own questions. | Students engage in open inquiry— determining all aspects of what is researched. Teacher acts as consultant. |

Figure 5.6 A Continuum for Gradual Release of Responsibility for Generating Questions

is also up to you to decide how quickly this happens. Implementing this continuum might happen slowly over the course of a year. It might happen more quickly, perhaps over the course of a unit of study.

How Do We Help Along the Way?

Some students may easily generate topics and strong guiding questions. Some students may need more support. Our observations can help us determine whether they need support and what that support may look like. If they do need some support, there are various ways we can support them as they work toward doing this on their own.

Determine the topic and questions students will pursue on earlier projects before releasing responsibility for this in later projects. For example, in a fifth-grade class studying the interdependent relationships in ecosystems, a teacher might use an inquiry chart to introduce the concept of ecosystems to students. The teacher provides basic questions for the chart that serve to build students' background knowledge: "What is the definition of an ecosystem? What are critical interactions or processes that occur in ecosystems? What are examples of ecosystems?" Later in the unit, the teacher might ask small groups to complete a second chart on a particular ecosystem the group chooses with questions they generate together. Toward the end of the unit, the teacher might ask individual students to choose an endangered ecosystem, generate their own questions about the impact of humans on that ecosystem, and then complete the chart on their own. When you determine the topic and questions early on in a school year or unit of study, you are providing a model for students to consider later and you are providing an opportunity for students to develop experience and see what happens when they research carefully chosen topics and questions. Then, when students take on more responsibilities later, they have a clear model of the process in mind.

Start with a "synthesis map." Before their students generate questions for research, my colleagues who teach at a middle school, Shannon and Micheline, ask their students to complete a graphic of what they already know about the topic. The students write the purpose for learning (which may be stated as a standard or learning target) in the middle of a large piece of paper. Then they jot notes about what they already know about the target or topic. The objective of this is for students to see what they already know and what they need to learn. At different points throughout the unit, the teachers ask the students to return to the synthesis map and jot down new learning with a different color of ink. Notice in the student's synthesis map in Figure 5.7 that the student has crossed out some details she later realized later were erroneous. This map helps students track their learning over time, but initially it may also help students generate questions for further research.

Provide time to explore first. Shannon and Micheline also provide time for students to look through sources—hard copies of texts and texts on the internet—before they zero in on a specific topic or questions. Students can more easily engage in asking questions if they have some prior knowledge of the topic. Providing time for students to explore and begin to wonder can be a huge help in this endeavor. Structure in the form of a series of prompts like "Search the words 'ecosystems endangered.' What ecosystems pop up? Why are they endangered? Which one are you most curious about? Why?" can be helpful.

Brainstorm and list topics and/or questions together. You might pose a content-area topic like "How did the environment influence the life of the Comanche Nation?" and then ask students, "What do we want to learn?" Acting as the scribe, you can list their questions on the board. Along the way, you can help them think critically about what makes a question worthy of research as well as manageable to research. When students pose simple questions like "What did they eat?" you might push them to think about higher-level questions like "How did they get their food?" and "How did their location influence what they ate?" If someone proposes a broad question like "What were the roles of the different family members?" you might ask them to narrow

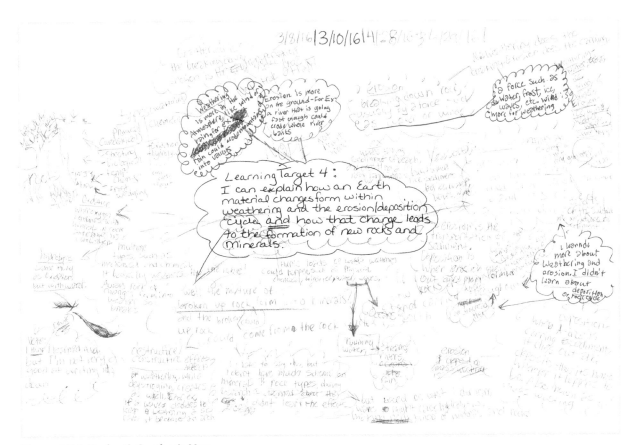

Figure 5.7 A Student's Synthesis Map

and refocus with a question like "How did the children rely on the environment to fulfill their role in the community?" Students can then choose questions from this list that they want to research further or use these questions as models when they develop their own.

Provide a continuous opportunity to model by choosing your own topic and questions. Engage in the process you are asking students to experience. Model for students how you chose a topic and determined questions. For example, Micheline chose a specific land formation to study the effects of erosion and weathering. She thought aloud for the students about why she was interested in that land formation; she brainstormed questions she could ask and then thought aloud about which three she would pick. At different points during the students' research, she returned to her topic and modeled different strategies, such as looking carefully at a powerful photograph and jotting down on her inquiry chart what she learned.

In mini-lessons, highlight the strategic thinking that happened in a conference with a student. My favorite way to teach is to help students share with their peers what they did to be strategic. In the case of identifying topics and questions, I might ask a student to come up front and place his inquiry chart on the document camera and think aloud about why he chose the questions he did or why he abandoned a question. Prompting the student to share particular details with questions like "What did you do to help you choose this topic?" or "What did you do when you figured out that question was too big?" makes these mini-lessons especially purposeful. If the student hesitates or struggles in describing their process, provide the language needed, for example: "When I came to confer with you, you were frustrated. Remember? You told me you thought there was just too much information to take notes about on your chart. What did you and I do to unpack that question?" When we engage students in thinking aloud in front of their peers about what they did to be strategic, we are nurturing these students' sense of "I can do this" and "I am a problem solver."

Observe students and plan mini-lessons at the point of need. When you observe your students and notice they are stuck somehow, consider what you might do during a mini-lesson to move them forward. For example, you might notice that several students have asked questions that are too big or broad to research well. In response, you might teach a mini-lesson on how to unpack a big question, creating smaller, more manageable questions. The chart in Figure 5.8 provides suggestions for mini-lessons based on your observations. You'll see in the examples in the chart that mini-lessons do not always have to be about reviewing or teaching helpful strategies; they're also opportunities for modeling with your own topic and questions or for highlighting what happened in a powerful conference with a student.

Confer, confer, confer. When you lean in to confer with students and notice they need support related to identifying strong topics or questions, consider the prompts or suggestions in Figure 5.9 for thinking aloud with the students if the prompt is helpful.

Figure 5.8 Suggestions for Mini-Lessons That Help Students Hone Their Guiding Questions

If you observe that . . .	Then provide a mini-lesson . . .

Students have chosen broad questions that are making research unmanageable.	• During a conference, help an individual student revise a question to make it manageable—not too big to research well. Then, during a mini-lesson, ask her to share how she did this with the whole class. This might include posting her initial question next to her unpacked question for students to view and consider.
	
	• Post a broad question for all the students to view and consider. Then pose questions for discussion like
	
	  ▪ *Why might this question be tricky to research?*
	
	  ▪ *What might I do to unpack this question or make this question manageable?*
	
	  ▪ *Should this be more than one question? Or is there a detail I can add that would make this question clearer?*
	
	  ▪ *How might I revise this question? Let's revise it together.*

Students are frustrated because they cannot find enough information to respond to a question.	• Ask a student who had this problem to speak to the class about what he did when he confronted this issue. Prompt the student to elaborate with questions like the following:
	
	  ▪ *What made you think you had a problem?*
	
	  ▪ *What did you do to try to solve this problem? How did that help?*
	
	  ▪ *Based on this experience, what did you learn about looking for information to answer a question?*
	
	• If you have noticed students are not using efficient search terms, discuss what a productive search looks like. You might create an anchor chart to remind students of how to structure searches.
	
	• With your own topic and question, model using poor search terms and stronger search terms to look for sources.
	
	• Talk with students about abandoning questions. Start a chart listing the students' suggestions for when to consider abandoning questions. Suggestions might include
	
	  ▪ when there are just a few details that answer the question
	
	  ▪ when you have consulted three to five sources and none seem to answer the question
	
	  ▪ when you know intuitively that it's not a good question.

Students are developing new questions in response to what they are learning.	With your own topic, think aloud about a new question that surfaced while you were reading a source and how you decided to do one of the following: • Save the question for later. • Add another column on your inquiry chart with this question. • Reject the question because it is not relevant enough or it was too broad or narrow.

Figure 5.9 Suggestions for Prompting and Thinking Aloud About Topics and Questions

Prompt	Suggestions for Thinking Aloud with Students If They Need Further Support
When you are thinking about a topic, what are you interested in that relates to our purpose for learning?	*Let's list a few possible topics together. When I think about this purpose for learning, I wonder about . . .*
What questions do you have about this topic?	*When I look at your synthesis map, I think one of my guiding questions might be . . .*
How can we unpack this question to make it manageable?	• *When I read this question, I noticed there were several different parts to the question . . .* • *When I read this question, I thought maybe this word right here included a lot of information.* • *Maybe we should look up the definition of that word and think about how we can write a question that gets at one part of that word (e.g., weathering or culture).*
What makes you think this question is not researchable?	*When you told me that . . . , I started thinking that this question might not be researchable because . . .*
What can you do if you think this question is not researchable?	*I think I might abandon this question or focus on just a part of it that . . .*

Teaching Students to Locate and Vet Sources for Relevance and Truthfulness

There are lots of sources "out there," and when we think about students locating sources on the web, what we mean by "out there" has become vast and sometimes unmanageable. Sources from the web come in many formats and text structures and they can be created by *anybody*. As researchers, students are tasked not only with finding relevant texts that they can make sense of but also with evaluating the accuracy and authority or truthfulness of those texts. We have to provide support along the way. Figure 5.10 is a continuum to use when we think about how to move students toward locating and vetting their own sources.

When we provide sources for students to use or choose from, we are also providing models for the type of and quality of sources students should look for on their own. When we provide only a few of the sources, we are launching students, freeing up cog-

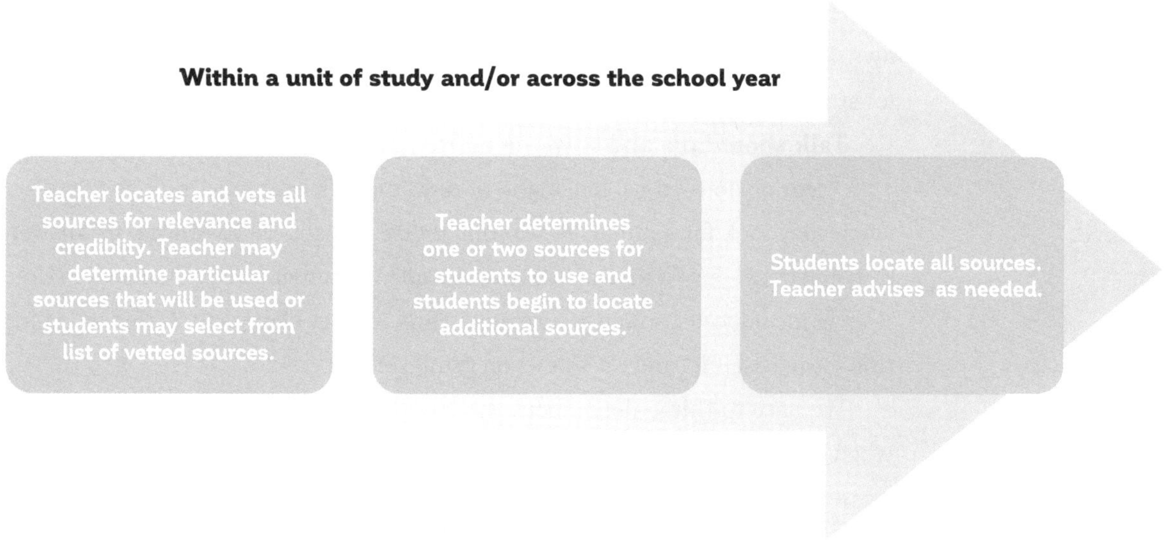

Within a unit of study and/or across the school year

Teacher locates and vets all sources for relevance and crediblity. Teacher may determine particular sources that will be used or students may select from list of vetted sources.	Teacher determines one or two sources for students to use and students begin to locate additional sources.	Students locate all sources. Teacher advises as needed.

Figure 5.10 A Continuum for Gradual Release of Responsibility for Vetting Resources

nitive energy to locate those additional sources. When we confer with students and ask questions about their choice of a particular source, we help them stay focused and we make it okay to accept or reject sources—a key step in moving research forward.

How Do We Help Along the Way?

Develop a set of sources from which students can choose. When my daughter was in sixth grade, she brought home a short research assignment on how submarines are structured and how they work. The assignment listed six questions about submarines that Anna needed to answer using the internet. Locating sources was up to her. As Anna searched for sources, she quickly became frustrated. The sources were complex texts primarily geared toward adult or more sophisticated readers, or the sources answered some questions and not others. I started to lean in and help. One question drove us nuts! We could not find an answer and we finally gave up. With little prior experience using the internet as a research tool and few experiences engaging with adequate sources online, Anna spent a lot of energy looking for sources and tackling sources. When she finished the assignment, she was exhausted and she did not understand that much more about the submarine.

I'm not saying students shouldn't experience locating their own sources. They should. My argument is that students need experiences with high-quality sources that have been carefully chosen by the teacher before they are sent off to locate their own.

These sources serve as models for the quality of sources students need to find on their own. These sources can be compiled as hyperlinks in a Word document and posted for students to access.

Talk about how and why you chose specific sources for students to use. It may seem obvious to us, but many of our students may not think about relevance when they look for sources. A *relevant source* is a source that helps us answer our research questions. With the fifth-grade students studying ecosystems, each time the teacher introduced a source to use on the first inquiry chart, she started by asking, "Is this source useful?" and "Why do you think so?"

We have to think aloud about the *truthfulness of a source*, too. We can do this when we present sources for students to use by asking questions related to authority, accuracy, purpose, and timeliness. Examples include:

* *How can we tell who or what organization developed this source?*

* *What do we know about this person or organization's experience related to this topic? Is this person or organization considered an authority in the field?*

* *Can we find these facts in more than one credible source? Or in more than one place?*

* *Why is the author writing/creating/including this source? How might that influence what the author includes in this source?*

* *When was this source created? Could the facts have changed? Or could new facts have emerged since then?*

The topic of evaluating sites for truthfulness is worthy of a much longer conversation and extensive professional reading. It is not an easy task and we as teachers do not always know how to answer these questions. If you can't answer these questions, maybe the source should not be used or perhaps you should try to find the answers. When I was working with seventh-grade students studying the Middle Ages, I kept coming across this one site—lordsandladies.org. There were no details about the author, but there was a link to email the webmaster, so I did. The person who responded included a short biography of the author's experience in distance learning and a list of several history-based sites for which the author had developed content. In addition, many of the facts that were listed were confirmed on other credible sites. As a result, I decided the site was credible and worthy of use.

I did this hesitantly, though. I'm still wondering if I should have used more credible sources. If the creator of the content on this site had been the National Geographic Society or the United States Holocaust Memorial Museum, I would have been more comfortable with my recommendation, knowing that members of these organizations actively and expertly vet content before it is made available on their site. My point here is that we need to at least think aloud for students about evaluating sources for truthfulness. One way to start is by asking students to identify the creators or developers of the sources they choose and to note what makes them think these institutions or individuals are credible. This may serve to quickly weed out sites that include information provided by anonymous authors.

Continue modeling with your own topic and questions, with a focus on how you choose sources. In the previous section, I mentioned modeling choosing your own topic and questions. You can continue to support students by thinking aloud about how you are locating and vetting sources for relevance and usefulness. I'm not suggesting that you engage in a huge research project on your own topic, but having your own topic and questions, for which you can locate texts, can serve as an easy way to pull everyone together and focus on a particular strategy.

Observe students as they locate their own sources and plan mini-lessons at the point of need. Figure 5.11 offers suggestions for mini-lessons you might provide based on what you observe during your conferences with individuals or small groups.

Confer, confer, confer. When you lean in to confer with students and notice they need support related to locating and vetting sources, consider the prompts and suggested language for thinking aloud in Figure 5.12.

Figure 5.11 Suggestions for Mini-Lessons That Help Students Locate Their Own Source

If you observe that . . .	Then provide a mini-lesson about . . .
Students are reading every text they find without considering how relevant the text is to the guiding questions.	• Explicitly teach students what it means to skim and scan and to read or reject. Choose a source that might or might not be helpful in answering questions for your own research topic. Think aloud for students about why you are choosing to read or reject this source after skimming and scanning. • Create an anchor chart that defines and reminds students what it means to skim, scan, read, or reject.

If you're trying to . . .	Use this strategy . . .
decide whether this article might be relevant or helpful to your research	**Skim:** systematically read key parts of a text—*title, headings, first sentence in each section, text features*
locate a section of the text that might be important to read closely	**Scan:** look for key words or phrases that are related to your questions
learn information that might be helpful in answering your questions and understanding your topic	**Read closely:** read and reread relevant sections of the text (e.g., the whole text, a section under one heading, a text feature)
stay focused on your topic and avoid spending time on unhelpful sources	**Reject:** decide not to read or view the source because it is not relevant or adequate

	• If you taught students how to use the THIEVES mnemonic to preview and make informed predictions as described in Chapter 3, discuss with students how this is a way to "skim" the text. • Model with a "cold" source. Locate a source that you think may have some relevance to your own topic and questions. Don't spend a lot of time preparing to model for the students. Instead engage in a "cold" read of sorts—modeling how you made sense of whether the text would be relevant to your topic of study.
Students are not evaluating sources.	• Explicitly teach students at least one key question to ask when they locate a source: ▪ *Who is the host or creator of the content of this source?* • Additional questions you might introduce: ▪ *Does the host of this site or the creator of the source have authority or expertise on this topic?* ▪ *What is the purpose of this site? How might that purpose influence what the host or creator includes in this source?* • With your own topic, model using the questions above for evaluating sources. • Highlight a conference with a student that focused on determining the developer of a source and deciding whether that developer was credible or not.

(continues)

Figure 5.11 Suggestions for Mini-Lessons That Help Students Locate Their Own Source *(continued)*

If you observe that . . .	Then provide a mini-lesson about . . .

Students are clicking on the first link that pops up in their search.	• Review the skim, scan, read, or reject strategy.
	
	• Over time, engage the students in keeping a running list of trusted sources, such as the Smithsonian national museums.
	
	• Explicitly teach students how to navigate the search engine results page (SERP). You might list reminders on a piece of chart paper and/or model thinking through links that pop up when you enter your own search terms. Suggestions to consider:
	
	  ▪ **Skip the sponsored results.** The first entries in the list may be "sponsored" results or an advertisement for a particular product, company, or institution. Skip these!
	
	  ▪ **Look for the organic results and then check out domain names.**
	    • *Do you recognize the domain name?*
	    • *Is this a reliable and relevant institution related to the government, education, or a trusted company?*
	
	  ▪ **Ask questions before you click.** Slow down and read the *title*, *link*, and *short description*. Does the information provided seem relevant or helpful?
	
	  ▪ **Provide a mini-lesson on noticing links that are sponsored and links that are organic.** You might post a SERP that includes advertisements or sponsored links at the top of the search results and ask students to notice the difference between these links and others further down. There is usually a clear line that divides the two types of links.

Students are searching with terms that are too broad or narrow.	• With your topic or a particular student's topic, think aloud about what happens when you search a term that is too broad or narrow. For example, in this image, notice the organic links in the SERP for the search terms "Grand Canyon + weathering." There's only one that might be helpful to students studying how chemical weathering has influenced the formation of the Grand Canyon. Search terms like "Grand Canyon + mechanical weathering."

Figure 5.12 Suggestions for Prompting and Thinking Aloud About a Source

Prompt	Suggestions for Thinking Aloud with Students If They Need Further Support
Let's look back at your question. What are words that might help us search for more useful information?	*When I looked back at your guiding question, there were a few key words that jumped out at me. (Name the words and explain why they are "key.") What if you did a search with those words?*
Why do you think this source is useful or not?	*Remember that when you are not sure a source is useful, you can start by skimming or systematically reading key parts of a text—title, headings, first sentence in each section, text features. Let's do this together right now.*
Who or what group created this source that you found? How did you figure that out?	*Let's go back and look at this source again. Maybe I can help you figure out who created or developed this source.*

Grappling with Texts, Synthesizing, and Taking Notes

In the beginning—at the start of the school year or a new unit of study, we may hold our students close as they engage in this process. The whole class may share a topic and questions, reading and taking notes from the same sources. Just as they need to take more control of identifying topics and questions and locating sources, they also need to take more control of reading and note taking. This does not mean we are leaving the scene, though. In the continuum in Figure 5.13, notice how the teacher is always present to provide some support along the way—even just as an adviser or consultant.

If we want to make sure students take risks with their learning or if we want to be there to support (not rescue) students as they take risks, we have to continue being present at various points during the research process. Shannon and Micheline's middle school students engage in ongoing research that occurs during class time and at home. Each day at the beginning of class, the students meet in small groups to talk through what they learned independently at home the night before, referring to their notes. Because the students are working on different topics, their conversations are about the process of their work, not the content. They also think aloud about their processes. This might include how they abandoned or unpacked a question. After these initial discussions, the teacher gives a quick mini-lesson, modeling a strategy she noticed the students need to use. She does this with her own topic. For example,

Within a unit of study and/or across the school year

With a common topic and questions, the teacher and students read a source and take notes together. Then students read and take notes from additional sources with teacher present to coach.

With his or her own topic and questions, the teacher models using various strategies to read, think, and take notes. Students research their own related topic and questions with teacher present to coach.

Students research a topic and questions with the teacher present to advise.

Figure 5.13 A Continuum for Gradual Release of Responsibility for Grappling with Texts

when Micheline noticed that some of the students were quickly abandoning relevant texts that they found too difficult, she modeled reading and making sense of a tricky text. With this new strategy in mind, the students returned to their research. As the teacher moved around the room, conferring at the point of need, she found a few moments to lean in and coach students as they grappled with tricky texts, reinforcing what she'd modeled during the mini-lesson.

How Do We Help Along the Way?

Develop a daily routine for research. Figure 5.14 illustrates what a daily routine for students engaged in more control of reading and taking notes from multiple texts might look like. This routine could happen whether students are using questions you all generated together or they are using questions they generated on their own and whether students are using sources you determined in advance or they are looking for their own sources.

For some students, research may need to happen only during class time. Sometimes our students lack access to sources at home or they may have trouble finding a place and time at home to engage in research. Some students need modifications

In small groups, students discuss what they learned on their own the night before and insights they gained about the research process. The teacher leans in to listen. At the end of the small-group discussion, the teacher highlights a few points students made.

The teacher provides a mini-lesson demonstrating a strategy the students need.

The students return to their research and the teacher confers, coaching at points of need.

The students set goals for what they will accomplish during their research at home and follow up that night.

Figure 5.14 A Potential Daily Routine for Research

that are available only in a school setting. If that's the case, class begins with students discussing their research from the previous class.

Revisit the skills of determining a topic and questions when necessary. Prior to implementing this routine, you will already have helped your students identify their topic and questions (see previous sections in this chapter) and begin to locate relevant and truthful resources. As you get into this daily routine of reading, synthesizing, and taking notes, however, you may find that you need to return to these two areas and provide more mini-lessons. For example, students may generate some very strong questions for a while, but then suddenly veer into asking questions that require an opinion rather than a factual explanation. A quick mini-lesson might help them refocus.

Coach students in discussing what and how they are learning. Part of independence is being able to listen to and learn from peers. The daily routine described earlier includes this component at the beginning of each day's class, and the conversations don't need to take more than a few minutes. Coaching students in this work will keep the conversations helpful, focused, and specific. Highlighting what one student did to problem solve during a conference with you serves as a model for the kinds of conversations we want students to have with each other. Leaning in and listening during the students' conversations is another way to support them. When I listen to students talking, I look for real communication by thinking about the following questions:

- What are they saying that reveals they are talking about *what* they learned as well as *how* they learned?

- Do their responses also reveal that they have been listening to their peer?

- Is there a back-and-forth to this conversation that builds meaning? Or does it sound like they are just taking turns?

Observe students and plan mini-lessons at the point of need. When you get as far as thinking about mini-lessons that would help students who are engaged in reading and note taking, here are a few suggestions. The lessons in Chapter 3 might be helpful, too. For example, if you observe that students are reading or viewing second and third sources without thinking about what they've learned in previous sources, you might review the coding strategy. In the suggestions in Figure 5.15, you will notice that I again recommend modeling with sources related to your own topic and questions or highlighting the thinking a particular student did during a powerful conference.

Figure 5.15 Suggestions for Mini-Lessons That Help Students Work with Texts

If you observe that . . .	Then provide a mini-lesson about . . .
Students are abandoning complex texts too quickly instead of grappling with and making sense of these texts.	• Introduce or review the coding strategy discussed in Chapter 3, Lesson Idea 4. With your own topic or a student's topic, model coding your thinking with a small section of a source. This may serve as a reminder to students that they need to push their understanding—not just look for details that are easy to understand. • Model with a "cold" source. Locate a source that you know is relevant to your topic of study but that you haven't spent a lot of time preparing beforehand. Think aloud about what is tricky in a source on your topic and what you do to grapple with a complex text—rereading, making sense of parts with a bit of struggle, or abandoning particular details because they are too complex. Students need to know that it's okay to use a small portion of the text or particular details that they make sense of without mastering the entire text.
Students are relying primarily on particular types of text (written text or photographs, for example) and not tapping a variety of useful sources.	• With your own topic, model using a source students are not tapping—diagrams, maps, video, and so on. Refer to Chapter 4 Figure 4.4 for tips on thinking aloud about what you learn from these features. • Ask students who have used a particular source that others are not tapping to share their experience with this source—how they located the source, why they decided to use the source, how they examined and learned from the source. • Start an anchor chart listing types of sources and tips for locating and examining them.
Students are reading without keeping their purpose in mind.	With your own topic, model reviewing your questions. Put a source on the document camera or project it in some way, and think aloud about details in the text and how these details helped you answer a question. This is a quick mini-lesson just to help students refocus.
Students may need to take notes in a different format in order to make meaning of what they are reading.	Highlight how particular students have modified the inquiry chart in some way to make it work for their research needs. For example, in one of the classrooms in which I've worked, one student who was studying types of weathering and erosion sketched a diagram of abrasion and plucking instead of writing about these two concepts. She found the sketches helped her think through each concept and then contrast the two.
Students are unsure of when they have enough information to answer a question.	Students probably have enough information if they are reading the same details they already have notes on over and over again. You might need to talk about this explicitly during a mini-lesson, or you might call on one student you conferred with about this to share his experience determining he had enough information.
Students are taking isolated notes on texts rather than continually thinking across texts and consulting notes they have already taken.	With your own topic, review notes you have already taken on one source, and then as you examine a second source, think aloud about what you learned from the previous source and what you took notes on. Make comments to the students about how you decided what to add to your notes based on previous notes you took.

Confer, confer, confer. When you're listening to a student during a conference, ask yourself these two questions:

* *Do I need to provide support in making sense of this one source?*
* *Is there an opportunity to provide support in thinking across texts?*

If students are struggling with the source in front of them at that moment, then provide support there. This support will vary depending on the student's response. You may need to help students closely read a small portion of text and think aloud together with the students. You may need to offer suggestions for how students might sketch instead of jotting. You may need to remind students of strategies they've learned like coding the text or thinking about their questions to help them focus.

If the students seem to be grappling productively with the text in front of them, then check in with the students about how they are thinking across texts. You might use the following prompts:

* *How does what you are learning from this source resonate with what you've learned from other sources?*

* *What have you thought about in your notes on previous texts as you have examined this source?*

* *What are you noticing across the texts?*

If you need additional prompts, consult the suggested prompts in the lesson ideas in Chapter 3.

A Few Closing Thoughts

Remember the two students I described in Chapter 2 who were researching the hedgehog and were so proud because they'd read a *whole* book on hedgehogs? Remember that when I asked them what they were going to write about, they hesitated and then responded, "We're going to write about the *whole* book"? When I think about this anecdote, I can't help but think there were multiple missed opportunities in this context for teaching and for learning. When students engage in their own research, there are an abundance of opportunities for teaching. The trick is to think about areas of learning we can provide a scaffold for during the research process like identifying topics and questions, locating and vetting texts, and grappling with complex texts while also thinking across those texts.

Assessing: Suggestions for Marking Progress

6

Recently I watched fourth-grade students presenting what they'd learned about how Native American tribes in California used natural resources in their everyday lives hundreds of years ago. As a class these students had studied one tribe together. They had clear guiding questions to drive their thinking about multiple sources and they used an I-chart to organize their notes. Then in pairs, they tackled another tribe—using the same guiding questions, consulting multiple sources, and completing another I-chart.

As I watched students present, I was amazed at how easily they talked about their assigned tribe's use of natural resources. Phrases like "natural resources" and "coastal and central valley region" fell out of their mouths effortlessly as they described what they learned. When needed, the students easily stepped away from their scripts and explained further. Several used hand gestures to support what they were saying. Joseph gesticulated as he explained the engineering and design of arrows. They were able to extend or clarify what their partners said. When their peers asked questions, the presenting students' responded thoughtfully, frequently drawing conclusions based on what they had learned about their tribe's use of natural resources.

The students' comments also included clues to their learning and thinking processes. Some referred to their sources with statements like "We got this information

141

from . . ." Makayla stated that she and her partner realized part of their presentation "needed more details" and then went on to share what they had discovered. Alicia, a dual language learner, shared an anecdote that started with "Well, when I was looking on one of the websites with both of my partners, I actually looked for where does this tribe live and it [the website] showed me they live in between the Miwok and Charlie's team's group, the Pomo." Alicia's comment reveals engagement with sources in a purposeful way and awareness of her role within the larger group of pairs studying the tribes. Two partners even paused to clarify with each other what they were saying. Vaann made a statement about their tribe's diet that his partner did not agree with. She reminded him of a source they'd read that helped them clarify their thinking.

As I observed these students, I couldn't help but be amazed by the wealth of learning they were revealing and how comfortable they seemed in their role as experts. They knew very little about this topic at the beginning of this unit of study. With their teacher's support, the students had built a pathway for learning and then *learned*. As a result, these students understand the world around them better. Not only are they more aware of how regional natural resources played a role in people's lives in California in the past, but they are awakening to how natural resources play a role in our world today. More importantly, they have a sense of how they can continue to learn.

A variety of of experiences contributed to students' learning. Their teacher, Nicole, and I corresponded during this unit of study, so as I watched these students, I had an idea of what had happened along the way. They'd had clear guiding questions. They'd read or viewed or listened to a variety of sources. They'd created anchor charts with key vocabulary and referenced them over and over again. They'd taken notes using multiple I-charts. They'd talked and talked and talked about their learning, and they wrote and wrote and wrote.

We've discussed most of these elements in earlier chapters, but there's one more piece of our work with multiple texts to discuss: assessment. In this chapter, we'll highlight the role of formative assessment in our work and consider ways to use summative assessment when necessary.

▌ Formative Assessment

In teaching the unit on Native Americans that opens this chapter, Nicole used what she learned about students each day—her own formative assessment—to adjust her instruction. She assessed by engaging in the following:

- listening to individual students or small groups talk about what and how they are learning from multiple sources

- looking closely at students' annotated texts and notes for evidence of thinking across texts

- reading students' writing (or assessing other artifacts) carefully and noticing how students have integrated ideas from multiple sources or determined that some sources are more useful or reliable than others.

Formative assessment is woven into the work in this book. Your decisions about what lessons to teach, how you confer with students, and when and how you release responsibility to the students are all informed by what you see and hear from them on a daily basis.

As we observe and notice what our students are taking on easily and what they are struggling with through conversations and in their written notes or responses, we need to make shifts in our instruction. For example, if you notice that students have chosen questions that are too big, making research unmanageable, then you might give a mini-lesson in which you and the students unpack a big question, brainstorming smaller related questions that would be just as helpful to research. If you notice that students are reading every source they find on a topic and not thinking about the relevance of a source, then you may need to plan a mini-lesson that explicitly teaches them to skim and scan and then read or reject. Planning mini-lessons in response to what you have noticed during conferences or large-group discussions can move students forward. For specific suggestions on what you might observe or listen for and mini-lessons you might implement in response, review the "If . . . Then . . . " charts in Chapter 5 (Figures 5.8, 5.11, and 5.15). In Chapter 5, I also explained in detail how we can confer with students—what we can say to elicit responses that reveal how they are being strategic and what content they are learning. Listening to individual students share their thinking is one of my favorite approaches to assessment because I learn so much and can teach what is helpful to that child in that moment.

Summative Assessments and Grading

For me, formative assessment is the most important type of assessment because it helps me gauge how my students are doing and what instructional moves I need to make next. However, many of us have to also think about summative assessments.

How do we evaluate the sum of a student's learning? And for some of us, another question is how do we *grade* students' use of multiple sources? The remainder of this chapter focuses on these questions with suggestions for your consideration.

Consider Your Rubrics or Checklists

Start by examining how you have evaluated students in the past. Do your rubrics or checklists have criteria related to students' use of multiple sources? Think back to the sources you or others have used to grade papers or presentations or projects in the past. Do any of the expectations address students' use of multiple sources?

In Figure 6.1, I've included very basic criteria related to using multiple sources that might be incorporated into a rubric or even included on a checklist. One or two criteria might be enough to add to the rubrics you already have. They are drawn from or align with national and state standards. They can be used to evaluate a smaller experience like a short response students wrote after they read and analyzed the first two of many sources, or they can be used to evaluate larger endeavors like students'

Grades 2–3	Grades 4–5	Grades 6–8
The student includes information from multiple sources.	The student integrates information from multiple sources in different formats (e.g., graphics, video clips, texts).	The student integrates information from a variety of sources in different formats (e.g., diagrams, video clips, maps, etc.).
The student cites details from more than one source.	The student refers to details in multiple sources as needed.	When appropriate, the student cites several pieces of textual evidence to support a point.
The student speaks or writes easily about a topic, combining details from more than one source at the sentence level in a way that makes sense to the audience.	The student is able to explain further as needed (orally or in writing), drawing on information learned from multiple sources in a way that makes sense to the audience.	The student speaks knowledgeably about the topic or writes fluently, revealing depth of knowledge.
The student addresses (orally or in writing) how important details in two or more texts are the same or different.	The student's presentation of information (orally or in writing) reveals an analysis of different authors' points of view.	The student is able to speak or write about her analysis of texts that may have similar or contrasting information or authors' points of view.
The student identifies new questions he has as he reads multiple sources on a topic.	Based on the student's initial experiences reading multiple sources, the student generates new questions and pursues answers in additional sources.	The student generates new questions and pursues answers in additional sources.

Figure 6.1 Sample Expectations for Students' Use of Multiple Sources

written research reports or the contents of a student debate or podcast. As you read these sample criteria, here are a few questions to consider:

- Which of these criteria do you already use?
- Which criteria would be helpful to add?
- How might the criteria be revised to align with the learning standards your school or district follows?

When you select one of these expectations, think about how you can unpack what this looks like for your students at different levels of performance. Levels of performance might include *attempting*, *approaching*, *meeting*, and *exceeding*. Start by thinking about what exceeding would look like. The descriptors or characteristics of these levels may be influenced by your curriculum, your students, the point you are at in the school year, and the standards your students are required to meet. In Figure 6.2, I have included an example of what these levels might look like for one of these expectations.

Expectation: "The student is able to explain further as needed (orally or in writing), drawing on information learned from multiple sources in a way that makes sense to the audience."

Exceeding	Meeting	Approaching	Attempting
When the student is asked a question, she easily draws conclusions based on multiple sources. She makes clear the reasoning behind her response—referring to information already presented or that she learned from one or more sources and has not already discussed. She recognizes and states clearly when she does not know the answer to a question.	When the student is asked a question, he draws mostly accurate conclusions based on multiple sources. He states the reasoning behind his response—referring to information he learned from one or more sources. He may use his notes as a tool to facilitate his thinking about how to respond to the question. His response is adequate, giving the person who asked the question a better understanding of the topic. He recognizes when he does not know the answer to a question.	When the student is asked a question, she answers the question in brief. She may refer to her notes as a tool to help her think or read from the notes. Her response is mostly relevant to the question.	The student attempts to answer the question. He is clearly trying to draw from his sources. His response may not answer the question adequately.

Figure 6.2 Descriptors for Levels of Performance in Grades Four to Five

Evaluate or "Grade" at Multiple Points During the Process of Reading and Thinking Across Sources

I'm hesitant to grade students' notes, inquiry charts, annotated sources, and so on. I really want them to use those as tools to facilitate their thinking, not as products that will be evaluated on their own. There are other products of learning that might be graded, though.

You might ask students to write a short response to one of the guiding questions after they have consulted just a few sources. This might be as short as a paragraph. Before they write, provide them with the rubric or other tool you will use to grade their response. In your prompt, include a reminder that you would like them to reveal how they used both sources. For example, with a group of third-grade students reading about simple machines, the prompt might look like the following:

> *Describe what you have learned about the function of the wedge.*
> *What is the purpose of a wedge? Be sure to include details you have*
> *learned from both sources.*

With a group of eighth-grade students studying the Jewish resistance during the Holocaust, a prompt for a short response might look like the following:

> *As a class we have defined courage as "the ability to do something*
> *that is difficult or dangerous and to persevere despite the risks*
> *or time it might take to reach a goal." Describe how members of*
> *the Jewish resistance revealed their courage. Be sure to include*
> *information you have learned from both sources.*

Another option is to ask students to transfer their learning to a separate set of sources. The sources you choose can continue building content knowledge related to a unit of study. My colleague Nicole, who teaches fourth grade, has made analyzing multiple sources a regular part of the homework she assigns each week and uses the students' completed homework as opportunities for summative assessment. One example is shown in Figure 6.3a–b. Notice how the students are asked to analyze a photo on Monday night, a text on Tuesday night, and then a second text on Wednesday night. On Thursday night, they are asked to draw a diagram using information from all three sources.

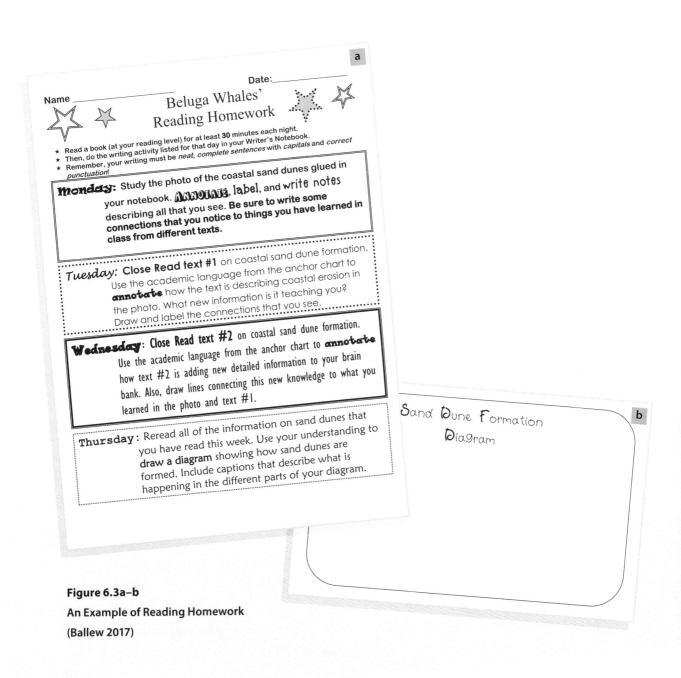

Figure 6.3a–b

An Example of Reading Homework

(Ballew 2017)

Position the Student as Your Partner in This Process

Sometimes we need help in recognizing what a student did to use multiple sources. We may not be familiar with all the sources that students consult, and it may not be easy to spot details from multiple sources in their written responses or when they are speaking. Students' self-evaluation can make this clearer to us when we assess their progress. Figure 6.4 is a portion of a rubric my colleague Karen developed for use with her third-grade students. Notice the kid-friendly statements.

Cross Text Synthesis	Not Yet	Starting To	Yes!
I can put together information on a common subtopic from different texts or parts of a longer text.			
I included information from each text to support my ideas.			

Figure 6.4 Cross Text Synthesis Self-Evaluation

An additional idea is to ask the students to write a quick reflection that focuses on how they made connections between sources during a particular lesson or experience. (You might need to model for students what this looks like.) They might write this on a sticky note and place it on their notes. In Figure 6.5, notice how the fourth-grade student drew arrows to the specific notes she discussed in her reflection.

You might use a prompt like one of the following:

* *On a sticky note, tell me about one connection you made between two sources today. Place this sticky note on your notes and turn them in to me.*

* *On a sticky note, write about information you found in more than one source that was similar or not similar. Put a star by details in your notes that reveal this.*

* *On a sticky note, tell me about what you noticed that was similar or not in the sources you consulted today.*

Tribe: Miwok	Source 1 www.fact-cards-califa.org	Source 2 www.warpath2pacehog.com	Source 3 www.
Which California region did the tribe live?	central california the miwok indens use what was around them.	• Central Valley Region of California	
What area or city would their location be close to now?	The city they were close to now is sacramento.	Northern t4xt	~tot 2
What types of houses did the tribe build and what natural resources were they made of?	The houses they builded warm in the ara of the mountian ranges. The miwok hoses were made from bark slabs shaped as a cone. Wich was could a teepe	The houses were made for different resons Somewere made for summer and winter.	Some other house they lived in was a winte pite house underground.
Did the homes have different purposes?	Some homes were made for winter like the thick ones.	Some homes were made for summer Like the tepees beause they are warmer.	~tot 2
What was the tribe's diet?	The food they ate were deer, elk, antelope, black grizzle, fox and, bob cats.	They also ate, rabbits, bevers, squirrls, wood rats they did not eat coyotes skunks, owls, snakes or	The also ate, acorns, berries, hazle nut and Pine nut.
What methods were used to obtain and collect their food?	Dear mrs ballew. What me and Joseph thought is that text1 gives us a lot of information but when we go to text 2 half of it Was the same but some Was not and the the stuff from text 2 that we did not know a bout we took that information u use it because We already have stuff from text 1, and text2 gave us More imformation —Makayle		e way they r the acid out the acorns s by boiling hem in water. text2
What tools did they create to catch their food?			
How did the tribe cook and prepare the various foods?			x2
How did tribe use their natural resources to create beauty? What was it used for?	jewelry Ma was made out of fruit. grass,		's jewlry they re were noce l ear romanments e totoos are y diffrent frm our's these days

Figure 6.5 Example of a Fourth-Grade Student Reflection

▌A Few Closing Thoughts

However we decide to evaluate the sum of students' learning, we have to be careful that we do not stifle the students' expression of what they have learned. The ultimate goal is for students to be able to speak or write knowledgeably about a topic or about their experience reading and thinking about more than one source, just as the students were doing in the scene at the beginning of this chapter. We also want them to attempt to transfer what they have learned without worrying about too many expectations and to be enthusiastic about reading more sources on that topic or others. While summative evaluation is good for filling in blanks in the grade book, it is also an opportunity to celebrate learning—at whatever level it has occurred.

Making This Work Your Own: Finding Opportunities for Reading Across Sources

7

Late in the spring Nicole and I spent some time talking with Makayla and Joseph, who had been in Nicole's third-grade class the previous school year and looped up with her to fourth grade that year. They'd spent two years reading multiple sources on nearly every topic they had studied. Recently, they'd collaborated to research and learn about one Native American tribe's use of natural resources in the past. I started the conversation by telling them I was in the process of finishing the manuscript for this book. When I asked if they had any advice for teachers who want to start teaching with more than one source, they looked at me incredulously. From the look on their faces, I expected them to say, "Is there any other way to learn?"

In the exchange below, Nicole and I help Makayla tease out what was so important to her about analyzing multiple sources:

Makayla: *I would say to my new teacher, "You need to give us more sources because one source doesn't give us all of the information."*

Sunday: *How do you know it doesn't give you all of the information you need?*

Makayla: (Pauses, thinking about the multiple sources she had read on the Miwok tribe.) *When we read source one, it only told us*

151

about the meat that the Miwok ate and how they hunted animals and cleaned the meat. But then I wanted to figure out more about the other foods they ate and the methods they used.

Nicole: *That's it! So you had a question!*

Makayla: (She smiles broadly. Now she understands what we are trying to get her to explain.) *Source one didn't answer my question.* (She pauses and then refers to another incident that occurred during their research on the Miwok.) *When we read source one, it said they [the Miwok] had to leach the acorns, and I asked, "Why did they have to leach them? Why didn't they just pop them off the oak trees and eat them?"*

Nicole: *What did you have to do?*

Makayla: *We had to find a second source!*

I'm laughing now, thinking about the patience Makayla had with us as she tried to explain her thinking. After two years, her use of multiple sources was a habit. In her mind, it was normal or natural to read a source, ask questions, and then find additional sources to answer those questions or to deepen her understanding of a topic.

In previous chapters I've made a lot of suggestions for teaching with multiple sources. I've also shared anecdotes from colleagues who have experienced this journey with me. In talking with these educators over the course of two years, what I have noticed is how they have started teaching with multiple sources on a *regular basis*. They have all found a way to make planning for and managing this type of instruction a *routine* part of their practice. Their actual instruction is similar. They all teach with very clear purposes for reading. They all vet the sources their students use and provide mini-lessons on how to make sense of and think across diverse sources. They all gradually release responsibility. However, the frequency with which this occurs, what subject it happens in, and how it fits into their district or school curriculum varies, depending on the context.

Two Models for Teaching with Multiple Sources Across the Year

Most of this book has been about what to do once you're working with multiple texts—but how do you work multiple texts into your plans for the year? What follows are two examples of what teaching with multiple sources might look like across the year. These models are based on what I learned from my colleagues.

As you look at these models, consider your own context for teaching. What are you already doing? Which (if any) of these options might be helpful to you? How might you add to your practice or modify it in some way to include more opportunities for students to read multiple sources?

Content-Area Units of Study

Do you teach specific science and social studies units of study? During the school year, as you move through planning for these units, think about how reading, viewing, and listening to multiple sources can be part of these units. Two of my colleagues teach with multiple sources for every science unit they teach. Their units are centered around district learning targets that are aligned with the Next Generation Science Standards. Another colleague combines the English Language Arts Standards and her state's science and social standards into integrated units of study. This gives her a major block of each school day to teach this unit. For each unit, she determines subtopics and creates sets of sources for those. What would work in your context for teaching? In which units of study across the year would teaching with multiple sources be manageable?

How many units? If you think teaching with multiple sources can happen on a regular basis during your content-area units of study, start by determining whether this will happen during every unit or as part of several units across the year. You might even look at each unit and decide which ones to teach with multiple sources. One colleague chose two social studies units and one science unit.

Here are suggestions for integrating sets of sources into each unit of study across the year:

- **Create a set of sources for the beginning of the unit to build background knowledge.** For example, if you are starting a unit focused on how humans can take steps to reduce the impact of natural hazards, your students might benefit from analyzing a set of sources that define and describe natural hazards.

- **Create a set of sources on harder subtopics to help students move forward in their learning.** Based on your previous experience teaching particular units or what you expect to happen based on what you know about your students, are there subtopics or concepts within that unit that your students will find particularly difficult to grasp? For example, when teaching about waves and their applications in technologies for information transfer, students might easily understand the concept of wavelengths but need more opportunities to consult sources that explain the concept of amplitude. During a unit on the American civil rights movement in the 1950s and 1960s, students may understand the idea of activists marching but not what it means to "sit in" as a form of protest. Create sets of sources for these subtopics.

- **Create a set of sources related to specific details in learning targets or standards that are an integral part of the unit.** If your units are aligned with the Next Generation Science Standards or the College, Career, and Civic Life (3C) Framework for Social Studies State Standards or your state's or district's learning standards, look at the standards themselves. Determine subtopics that might be better understood if students had an opportunity to experience analyzing multiple sources on that subtopic. In one district, the learning target was the following:

I can explain how an Earth material changes form within the weathering and erosion/deposition cycle and how that change leads to the formation of new rocks and minerals.

The teachers, my colleagues, tasked the students with unpacking this standard by asking themselves, "What do I need to know to be able to do this?" The list of subtopics the students generated became their purposes for locating sources and carefully reading, listening to, or viewing those sources.

- **Create a set of sources that specifically support the culminating project or performance task.** Ideally, a final project or task would integrate learning from across the unit, but there may be a place for a specific set of sources related to the project. For example, in a fifth-grade class studying American explorers, the students studied the economies of European nations, the many reasons for exploring the new continent, and so forth. For the culminating project, though, they studied one explorer's goals, achievements, and impact in detail. While they used the background knowledge they had developed on the broader topics, a set of sources on that particular explorer also supported this endeavor.

- **If you teach with a textbook, pick a subsection of that text and then locate related sources.** As described in Chapter 2, textbooks can be both dense and vague at the same time. If you've been using a textbook and would like to spur students' interest in a topic, pick a section of text in the textbook that could use a more thorough explanation. Then look for sources that build on the information in this section. For example, if the textbook includes general details about how American colonists did not honor treaties they made with Indian tribes, look for a source that goes into more detail about what happened with one particular treaty.

Small-Group and Whole-Group Reading Instruction

Several of my colleagues have made teaching with multiple sources a regular part of their reading instruction. Some meet with small groups while other students work independently. One is a reading specialist who pulls students from multiple classrooms into a group for instruction. Others lead whole-group reading lessons. Some of the teachers have a mandated source like an anthology their district requires them to use or a curriculum of sorts that includes themes for instruction. Others choose engaging, high-interest topics.

How often? If using multiple sources fits your context for teaching, decide how often you can do this. Once a quarter? Once a month? Every other week? All the time? As you determine how often you can commit to using multiple sources on a topic, here are a few suggestions to consider:

- **Pair up outside sources with a source you are required to use or other sources you already use.** Look at the informational texts you already use or are required to use. Find one or more additional sources on the same topic.

- **Gather sources on particular current events.** Do you subscribe to a classroom magazine? Choose a feature article from the magazine and then locate additional sources. Or visit a site like Scholastic News or Newsela and choose an article. Then Google the topic of that article to find additional sources.

- **Pair fiction and nonfiction.** If you teach with particular short stories, consider nonfiction sources that might help students build background knowledge that would be helpful in understanding the story or parts of the story better. Then develop a related set of sources.

- **Set parameters to make this manageable.** It might be helpful to list for yourself what should be included in a set of sources. As I shared earlier, a colleague and I found it helpful to commit to finding one text, one diagram, and one video clip for each topic. This made developing sets of sources much easier.

A Few Closing Thoughts

It's a delight to see the excitement of students like Makayla and Joseph when they suddenly see the connection between the details in two sources (see Figure 7.1). Or when they understand a first source better because of something the author stated in a second or third source. Or when they have a question while reading a source and realize they need *another source* to help them answer that question. Their excitement in the moment is exhilarating, but what this means for their future is even more thrilling: These students are learning that they can satisfy their curiosity about the world. They are forging their own paths in learning. They are thinking for themselves. Are there any higher goals than these in our work as educators? This is messy work, but it is fascinating and powerful work. I've been immersed in teaching with multiple sources for years now, but I see kids making fresh discoveries every time I'm in a classroom. I hope that, as you give it a go in your classrooms, you'll share your experiences—you can find me online (www.Sunday-Cummins.com) and on Twitter (@SundayCummins). I'm looking forward to learning with you and from you!

Figure 7.1 Makayla, Joseph, and Their Research

References

Adler, David A. 2008. *Heroes for Civil Rights*. New York: Holiday House.

———. 2015. *Simple Machines: Wheels, Levers, and Pulleys*. New York: Scholastic.

"African Elephant." 2014. *National Geographic Kids*. April 2. http://kids.national geographic.com/animals/african-elephant/#african-elephant-mud-family-baby.jpg.

Andrews, Evan. 2013. "8 Reasons It Wasn't Easy Being Spartan." History. March 5. www.history.com/news/history-lists/8-reasons-it-wasnt-easy-being-spartan.

Burleigh, Robert. 2015. *Trapped! A Whale's Rescue*. Watertown, MA: Charlesbridge.

Butterfield, Moira. 2009. *Medieval Lives: Knight*. Mankato, MN: Smart Apple Media.

"Can You Ride a Sound Wave?" 2017. Wonderopolis. Accessed August 24. https://wonderopolis.org/wonder/can-you-ride-a-sound-wave.

Collard, Sneed B., III. 2015. *Fire Birds: Valuing Natural Wildfires and Burned Forests*. Missoula, MT: Bucking Horse Books.

Culligan, Tricia. 2016. "Another Earth?" Scholastic News. October 14. http://magazines.scholastic.com/Top-News/2016/10/another-earth.

Cummins, Sunday. 2015. *Unpacking Complexity in Informational Texts: Principles and Practices for Grades 2–8*. New York: Guilford Press.

"Drone Control." 2015. Scholastic News. December 1. http://magazines.scholastic.com/news/2015/12/Drone-Control.

Farris, Christine King. 2003. *My Brother Martin: A Sister Remembers Growing Up with the Rev. Dr. Martin Luther King Jr.* New York: Simon & Schuster Books for Young Readers.

Fimrite, Peter. 2005. "Daring Rescue of Whale off Farallones / Humpback Nuzzled Her Saviors in Thanks After They Untangled Her from Crab Lines, Diver Says."

SFGate. December 14. www.sfgate.com/bayarea/article/Daring-rescue-of-whale -off-Farallones-Humpback-2557146.php.

Groover, Shilo. 2005. Letter to the editor. *ByGeorge! GW's Faculty, Staff, and Community Newspaper*, October 19. www2.gwu.edu/~bygeorge/oct1905/letter .html.

Haskins, Jim. 2005. *Delivering Justice: W. W. Law and the Fight for Civil Rights.* Cambridge, MA: Candlewick Press.

Hoffman, James V. 1992. "Critical Reading/Thinking Across the Curriculum: Using I-Charts to Support Learning." *Language Arts* 69 (2): 121–27.

"How Can You Get a Bird's Eye View?" 2017. Wonderopolis. Accessed August 24. https://wonderopolis.org/wonder/how-can-you-get-a-birds-eye-view.

Hoyt, Linda. 2008. *Revisit, Reflect, Retell: Time-Tested Strategies for Teaching Reading Comprehension.* Portsmouth, NH: Heinemann.

Jenkins, Martin. 2003. *Grandma Elephant's in Charge.* Cambridge, MA: Candlewick Press.

Johnson, Rebecca L. 2003. *Weather and Climate.* Washington, DC: National Geographic Society.

"Last Look: James Baker on Saving the Elephants." 2017. CNN video, 2:20. January 9. Posted on MSN. www.msn.com/en-us/video/tunedin/last-look-james-baker-on -saving-the-elephants/vp-BBy5r4q.

Lee, Russell. 1939. Photograph of segregated water cooler in Oklahoma City, Oklahoma. Farm Security Administration. July. Library of Congress. http://www .loc.gov/pictures/item/2017740552/.

Malory, Thomas. 2015. *Le Morte D'Arthur: King Arthur and the Knights of the Round Table.* San Diego: Canterbury Classics.

Manz, Suzanne Liff. 2002. A Strategy for Previewing Textbooks: Teaching Readers to Become THIEVES. *The Reading Teacher* 55 (5): 434.

National Council for the Social Studies (NCSS). 2013. *College, Career, and Civic Life (C3) Framework for Social Studies State Standards: Guidance for Enhancing the Rigor of K–12 Civics, Economics, Geography, and History.* Silver Spring, MD: National Council for the Social Studies.

NGSS Lead States. 2013. *Next Generation Science Standards: For States, By States.* Washington, DC: The National Academies Press.

Reflections: Ancient Civilizations. 2007. Orlando: Harcourt School Publishers.

San Diego Zoo. 2011. "Elephants." YouTube video, 3:15. April 13. www.youtube.com /watch?v=oH4Ml8vxW8E.

"Saving Africa's Elephants." 2017. Scholastic News. January 18. http://magazines .scholastic.com/news/2017/01/Saving-Africa-s-Elephants.

Simon, Seymour. 2013. *Seymour Simon's Extreme Oceans*. San Francisco: Chronicle Books.

Sis, Peter. 1991. *Follow the Dream: The Story of Christopher Columbus*. New York: Alfred A. Knopf.

Stiles, Daniel. 2016. "Cracking Down on the Illegal Ivory Market Is Key to Saving the Elephants." *Guardian via Newsela*, November 19. https://newsela.com/read /save-elephants-plan/id/24303/.

Tieck, Sarah. *Algonquin*. Minneapolis, MN: Big Buddy Books, 2015.

Tomecek, Stephen M.. *Machines Make It Move*. Washington, DC: National Geographic Reading Expeditions. 2003.

Tonatiuh, Duncan. 2014. *Separate Is Never Equal: Sylvia Mendez & Her Family's Fight for Desegregation*. New York: Abrams Books for Young Readers.

Tran, Lina. 2017. "An Earth-like Atmosphere May Not Survive Proxima b's Orbit." NASA's Goddard Space Flight Center. July 31. https://nasa.gov/feature /goddard/2017/an-earth-like-atmosphere-may-not-survive-proxima-b-s-orbit.

"Trinity of Energy." 2017. Beached-aaz. Accessed August 24. http://beached-aaz .wikispaces.com/trinity+of+energy.

U.S. National Park Service. 2016. "The Role of Wildland Fires in an Ecosystem." Newsela. December 11. https://newsela.com/read/govt-science-wildfires/id/24569.

USDA Forest Service. 2013. "Black-Backed Woodpeckers and Fire." YouTube video, 5:00. August 6. www.youtube.com/watch?v=Q1UnMDGqG_4.

"Where Is Tornado Alley?" 2017. Wonderopolis. Accessed August 24. https: //wonderopolis.org/wonder/where-is-tornado-alley.

"Why Does My Voice Sound Different on a Recording?" 2017. Wonderopolis. Accessed August 24. https://wonderopolis.org/wonder/why-does-my-voice-sound-different -on-a-recording.

Yolen, Jane. 1992. *Encounter*. San Diego: Harcourt Brace Jovanovich.